M000238983

PHOENIX THEN AND N

You can find most of the key
in the book on this outline m

Numbers in red circles refer to the pages where sites appear in the book.

* The map is intended to give readers a broad view of where the sites are located.
Please consult a tourist map for greater detail.

PHOENIX

THEN AND NOW®

First published in the United Kingdom in 2017 by
PAVILION BOOKS
an imprint of Pavilion Books Company Ltd.,
43 Great Ormond Street, London WC1N 3HZ, UK.

"Then and Now" is a registered trademark of Salamander Books Limited,
a division of Pavilion Books Group.

© 2017 Salamander Books Limited, a division of Pavilion Books Group.

This book is a revision of the original *Phoenix Then and Now* first produced in 2005 by
Salamander Books, a division of Pavilion Books Group.

Copyright under International, Pan American, and Universal Copyright Conventions.
All rights reserved. No part of this book may be reproduced or transmitted in any form
or by any means, electronic or mechanical, including photocopying, recording, or by any
information storage-and-retrieval system, without written permission from the copyright holder.
Brief passages (not to exceed 1,000 words) may be quoted for reviews.

All notations of errors or omissions should be addressed to Salamander Books,
43 Great Ormond Street, London WC1N 3HZ, UK.

ISBN-13: 978-1-911216-46-9

Printed in China

10 9 8 7 6 5 4 3 2 1

ACKNOWLEDGMENTS

The authors would like to thank Victoria and Marcus Scharbach and Cathleen, John, and
Judy Akers. A special dedication to the McCulloch brothers (James and William), whose early
commercial photography in Phoenix made many of the wonderful historical images possible.
Also to Herb and Dorothy McLaughlin, who purchased all of the original McCulloch photographs
and later donated those and all of the images they took of Arizona over the years to the Arizona
State University Library. Thanks to all the individuals and companies that granted access to
buildings, rooftops, etc. Without this access, many of the "now" photographs would not have
been successful comparisons to their "then" counterparts. Thanks to the staff of the Arizona
Collection at Arizona State University, Tom Canasi, Amy Douglass, Christine Moore, the staff
of the Arizona Room at the Phoenix Burton Barr Central Library, the staff of the Scottsdale
Historical Society, Carol St. Clair, and Anna Uremovich. John would especially like to thank John
Jacquemart for the lead. Paul Scharbach can be reached at paul@arizonaimages.com.

PICTURE CREDITS

The publisher wishes to thank the following for kindly supplying the photographs that appear in
this book:

Arizona Biltmore Resort: 92
Arizona Historical Society Museum at Papago Park: 10 [AZH-77.57.01], 18 [AZH-79.95.140], 20 [AZH-
    1975.48.07C], 58 [AZH-1976.125.07], 62 [AZH-81.164.02], 70 [AZH-1992.78.139], 74 [AZH-89.113.01]
Arizona Historical Society/Tucson: 22 [AHS #23,713], 64 [AHS #PC180-F248-0222]
Arizona Jewish Historical Society: 76
Arizona State University Libraries: Forrest Doucette Photographs, Arizona Collection, Arizona
    State University Libraries: 36; Herb and Dorothy McLaughlin Collection, Arizona State University
    Libraries: 48, 56, 84, 88, 124; McCulloch Brothers Photographs, Herb and Dorothy McLaughlin
    Collection, Arizona State University Libraries: 8, 16, 24, 28, 32, 34, 38, 40, 42, 44, 50, 82, 86, 94, 142
Getty Images: 122, 132, 134
Glendale Arizona Historical Society: 102, 104
Jacques Family, Glendale Arizona Historical Society: 100
Jeremy Rowe Vintage Photography: 14, 30, 46, 66, 68, 98, 126
Kennilworth School: 72
Library of Congress: 96
Mesa South West Museum: 90, 136, 138
McClintock Collection, Arizona Room, Phoenix Public Library: 12, 26, 60, 78, 80
Scottsdale Historical Society: 130
St. Mary's Basilica: 52, 54
Tempe Historical Museum: 106, 108, 110, 112, 114, 116, 118, 120

All "now" photographs were taken by Karl Mondon, except for pages 23, 29, 31, 43, 51, 57, 67, 69, 73,
79, 83, 91, 93, 99, 101, 103, 105, 113, 119, 121, 127, 137, 143, which were taken by Paul Scharbach.

PHOENIX
THEN AND NOW®

JOHN H. AKERS AND PAUL SCHARBACH

PAVILION

Washington Street and Central Avenue, c. 1940   p. 8

First and Washington Streets, c. 1900   p. 12

Hotel San Carlos, c. 1930   p. 32

Monroe at First Street and Central Avenue, c. 1949   p. 38

First Avenue from Jackson, c. 1933   p. 40

Phoenix Union Station, c. 1926   p. 44

St. Mary's Catholic Basilica, c. 1920   p. 54

Phoenix High School, c. 1917   p. 60

Arizona Capitol, c. 1920   p. 68

The Ellis-Shackelford House, c. 1920   p. 74

Phoenix Indian School, c. 1912   p. 80

Brophy College Preparatory School, 1928   p. 88

Tovrea Castle at Carraro Heights, c. 1935   p. 94

Papago Park, c. 1930   p. 98

Glendale State Bank, c. 1910   p. 102

Mill Avenue Bridge, 1933   p. 106

Jokake Inn / Paradise Inn, c. 1930   p. 128

Main Street, Mesa, 1959   p. 132

PHOENIX

THEN AND NOW INTRODUCTION

While Phoenix might still be young compared to most large American cities, its location has a fascinating story that stretches back well before the city was founded. Hundreds of years before enterprising settlers established Phoenix in central Arizona's Salt River Valley, a group of Native Americans, who archaeologists call the Hohokam, made their homes here and built miles of irrigation canals for a series of villages. In the mid-1400s, they suddenly and mysteriously abandoned everything and moved away.

There were no settlements in the area for a few hundred years after that. The United States captured the region in the Mexican-American War in 1848, but it wasn't until 1865, when the U.S. military initiated the development of the Salt River Valley, that people decided to establish a town here. Once the army established Camp McDowell on the valley's east end, people flocked to the region to claim the rich farmland, sell food to the fort and nearby mining towns, and make a living.

Phoenix was the first town to get started and it became the center of the Salt River Valley's growth. After Phoenix's founders rehabilitated the Hohokam canals, they named their town after the mythical firebird that regenerated itself. In 1870 they established a formal town site that today is between Seventh Avenue and Seventh Street, and Van Buren and the railroad tracks. Today this is Phoenix's downtown, a district of skyscrapers, schools, government buildings, churches, hotels, and warehouses in a variety of architectural styles, such as Art Deco and Mission Revival.

Phoenix became the seat of the newly created Maricopa County in 1871, although the town did not incorporate until 1881. Once the railroad connected Phoenix to the rest of the country in 1887, the town leaders started to assert themselves. They lobbied for Phoenix to become the territorial capital in 1889 and completed a new Neoclassical Revival capitol building in 1900. Phoenix remained the capital when Arizona gained statehood in 1912.

Several outlying farming towns have become part of metropolitan Phoenix. Tempe, named for the fertile Vale of Tempe in Greece, started on the south bank of the Salt River around 1870. The Mormons started Mesa to the east in 1878. Far out in the northwest, land developer W. J. Murphy founded the town of Glendale in 1892, naming it after Glendale in California; he banned alcohol there to ensure that he would attract dependable settlers. Northeast of Phoenix, the tiny village of Scottsdale was established in 1894, near where former army chaplain Winfield Scott first homesteaded.

The inhabitants of the valley dreamed of creating an agricultural empire, but water was a big problem in the early years. Salt River floods destroyed irrigation systems in the 1890s, then droughts followed. Completed in 1911, the Roosevelt Dam ensured the water supply and the local economy blossomed as a result. In the 1920s, skyscrapers rose up in Phoenix's downtown, and new resorts, such as the Arizona Biltmore, sprung up in the surrounding desert to attract tourists.

The Phoenix area grew steadily through the 1940s. World War II dynamically transformed the valley from a place of small farming towns to a sprawling metropolis. Attracted by the region's sunny climate, the government built military bases, especially airfields to train pilots. Those servicemen returned with their families after the war seeking jobs and housing, joining in the nation's big postwar migration to the "Sun Belt." Home builders met the insatiable demand for houses by building farther away from the downtown area and creating suburban neighborhoods. The open spaces between the towns eventually disappeared.

Businesses were attracted to the area by the burgeoning work force, and new shopping centers enticed shoppers away from the old downtown. Many offices moved from Phoenix's downtown for new skyscrapers in the Uptown district of Central Avenue. Downtown Phoenix suffered from the relocation of businesses and movement away from residential buildings, but things started to change in the 1970s. Small businesses were attracted by the cheap rents, and residents were drawn to historic neighborhoods. Phoenix preserved the last of its original houses in a block-long district called Heritage Square. In the 1990s the city also built two sports venues: America West Arena (now Talking Stick Resort Arena), home of the National Basketball Association's Phoenix Suns, and Bank One Ballpark (now Chase Field), home of the 2001 baseball world-champion Arizona Diamondbacks. Today Phoenix's historic heart, the Downtown Phoenix district, is enjoying a renaissance thanks to the arrival of the biotechnology industry, the Arizona State University Downtown Phoenix campus, and the desire of many to experience urban living in new condominiums.

The valley's other cities also underwent similar ebbs and flows of suburbanization, downtown decline, and rebirth. Tempe has transformed the area around the usually dry Salt River bed with a lake. Tempe's Mill Avenue district and its turn-of-the-twentieth-century commercial buildings cater to university students and shoppers alike. Mesa built a new performing arts center to help revitalize its downtown. Glendale's downtown includes Arizona's largest antiques district. Scottsdale attracts tourists and winter residents to its Western-themed downtown and art galleries. The introduction of METRO, a 26-mile light rail system that began operations in 2008, has led to rapid urban development in downtown Phoenix, Tempe, and Mesa. Every year thousands of people move into or visit the Phoenix area. Phoenix is now America's sixth largest city and the region has over four million people.

c. 1940

WASHINGTON STREET AND CENTRAL AVENUE

This busy intersection was the geographical center of downtown Phoenix

LEFT: The intersection of Washington Street and Central Avenue, shown here around 1940, was considered Phoenix's "peak land-value intersection," the geographic center of the original Phoenix town site. City residents and visitors from the outlying areas would flock here on Saturdays to shop and see movies, rituals preserved until the 1950s. In the center is the Goodrich Building, which, for many years, housed a Walgreen Drugs complete with a lunch counter. Down Central can be seen the Heard Building (with the radio tower), the Hotel San Carlos, the Security Building (with the ornate tower), and the Hotel Westward Ho. Crossing Central is one of Phoenix's public buses, which completely replaced Phoenix's streetcar system by 1947.

ABOVE: This is probably one of the most changed intersections in Phoenix. CityScape Phoenix, a high-rise mix of residential, retail, and office space, straddles both sides of Central Avenue in the foreground. Begun in 2008 through a redevelopment agreement with the City of Phoenix, the project replaced the former Patriots Park—an early downtown revitalization project built in the 1970s. The Goodrich Building is gone, replaced by the towering Renaissance Square. To the right across Washington Street is the One North Central Office Tower. Formerly the Phelps Dodge Tower, Freeport-McMoRan acquired the mining company in 2007 and moved out of the building. The Renaissance Hotel is just behind and the tower behind that is Arizona's tallest building, the Chase Tower. Down Central Avenue to the left, most of the buildings from the previous view are still standing. Tracks for the region's new light rail system, METRO, are visible on Central Avenue.

c. 1897

WASHINGTON STREET

The place for parades, marches, and funeral processions

ABOVE: This is the north side of Washington Street, near First Avenue, in the late 1890s. Washington Street, which ran through the center of the original Phoenix town site, was the place for parades, marches, and funeral processions. On the right-hand side of the street, in the far distance, is the Ford Hotel (see the Ford sign). The tall structure to its right with the metal point is the Fleming Building, home to the Phoenix National Bank. The next building down is the Monihan Building. The street also housed retail establishments—the white building in the center of the photo is the Dorris-Heyman Furniture Company, and Alboehmer's Drug Store and a watch store are on the right.

ABOVE: The Wells Fargo skyscraper and plaza now sits on the block where the Fleming Building and the Ford Hotel once stood. Before the demolition of both old buildings around 1970, the Fleming continued to look much the way it used to, but the Ford was barely recognizable. The twenty-seven-story Wells Fargo tower, which first belonged to First Interstate Bank, was completed in 1971. It was the first of three major skyscrapers to go into the downtown in the 1970s. All were banks and they represented the commitment of the local financial industry to downtown when so many other corporate headquarters were still moving to the Uptown section of Central Avenue. Wells Fargo bought out First Interstate in 1996.

c. 1900

FIRST AND WASHINGTON STREETS

One of the most intact blocks left in downtown Phoenix

LEFT: This is the north side of Washington Street, between First and Second streets, around 1900. To the far left is the Ezra W. Thayer Hardware Store, an important early Phoenix business. To the right is Bob's Place Saloon. Next door is the Goldwater Store, which opened in this location in 1899 and was owned by the father of future Arizona Senator Barry Goldwater. The two-story building to the right is the Fry Building. Built in 1885, it was designed by prominent architect James Creighton. The Plaza Boarding House was on the second floor. The building's owners remodeled it around 1929, changing its appearance. To the far right, on the other side of Second Street, is the Dennis Block.

ABOVE: Although some of the buildings on Washington between First and Second streets have changed, this is still one of the most intact blocks left in downtown Phoenix. A modern multi-story building now sits just to the left of the old Thayer Building. Several of the storefronts, including the Thayer Building, now feature restaurants, taking advantage of their close location to the Talking Stick Resort Arena (formerly American West Arena and the U.S. Airways Center)—home of the NBA's Phoenix Suns—as well as being on the METRO light rail system (opened in 2008). The arena's construction brought in many new businesses, including Majerle's Sports Grill in the Fry Building, the oldest-surviving commercial building left in Phoenix. The grill is named for and owned by current college basketball coach and former Phoenix Suns player Dan Majerle, who helped the team reach the NBA championship finals in 1993.

MARICOPA COUNTY COURTHOUSE
Built on the site of the original county courthouse

BELOW: Opened right before the stock market crash of 1929, the combined Maricopa County Courthouse and Phoenix City Hall is pictured here in 1930. The building was the result of a partnership between the county and the city. Phoenix had been the seat of Maricopa County since its creation in 1871, and the first county courthouse stood on this very spot near the center of town. That building came down in 1928 to make room for this one. Both the county and the city contributed to the construction, and each

hired its own architect. The county hired Edward Neild, an architect from Shreveport, Louisiana, to design its portion of the building. The City of Phoenix hired the prolific local firm of Lescher and Mahoney to design the western side. Together the architects came up with a building that combined elements of the Neoclassical, Spanish Colonial Revival, and Art Deco styles.

1930

BELOW: The Maricopa County Superior Court still uses the building, following the renovation of its historic courtrooms. One of the courtrooms witnessed a trial that had national impact. The county convicted Ernesto Miranda of rape, kidnapping, and robbery, but the U.S. Supreme Court overturned the conviction in 1966 because Miranda was not told that he had the right to legal counsel under the Sixth Amendment. As a result, police now read suspects their Miranda Rights. Fittingly, the Maricopa County Justice

Museum opened in a sixth-floor cell block in the building in 2012. No longer Phoenix City Hall—city officials moved to the new twenty-story city hall across the street in 1994—the Phoenix Police Museum now calls the building home. Established in another downtown location in 1995, the museum tells the story of law enforcement in Phoenix from territorial times to the present.

c. 1925

HEARD BUILDING

Home to the *Arizona Republic* and the
Phoenix Gazette from 1920 to 1948

LEFT: The Heard Building, on Central Avenue south
of Monroe, in the 1920s. Dwight Bancroft Heard was
probably one of the biggest movers and shakers in
Phoenix's early history. Appropriately, his eight-story
building was Phoenix's first skyscraper and one of
its tallest buildings for many years. Heard was a
successful Chicago businessman who moved out to
Phoenix in 1895 to improve his health. He joined his
former boss and father-in-law A. C. Bartlett in the
Bartlett-Heard Cattle Company and founded the Dwight
B. Heard Investment Company. Heard found success
and built a couple of skyscrapers, including the Heard
Building in 1920. He also bought a languishing Phoenix
newspaper called the *Arizona Republican*, changed its
name to the *Arizona Republic*, and made it the state's
largest newspaper and strongest booster. Heard died
in 1929.

RIGHT: The Heard Building, which was modernized in the late 1930s, has probably been seen by more people worldwide than any other Phoenix structure. Alfred Hitchcock's 1960 shocker, *Psycho*, opens with a shot of this building. For many years the Heard had a large radio tower on top for local station KTAR (part of which stands for the *Arizona Republic*, Dwight Heard's old newspaper). The tower is still there in the movie but was later taken down, leading many people to think that the Hotel Westward Ho (which still has a tower on top) got the cameo. This might be why director Gus Van Sant features the Westward Ho in his 1998 remake of Hitchcock's classic. Phoenix developer Chris Rudel purchased the building in 2000 and has gradually restored the exterior and sought to give the first floor more "street presence." Located near the Arizona State University Downtown Phoenix Campus, the university uses part of the building.

c. 1930

HOTEL ADAMS / RENAISSANCE PHOENIX DOWNTOWN HOTEL
The first hotel on this site was built in 1896

LEFT: Every city had its notable big hotels, and the Adams was legendary in Phoenix. Here is the second hotel with that name, located at First Street and Adams, about 1930. The original Hotel Adams was a massive 200-room structure, built in 1896, that quickly became a popular meeting place for political leaders and businessmen. Due to its mostly wooden structure, it burned down in one of Phoenix's most spectacular fires on May 17, 1910. The second Adams was constructed on the site of the first within a year or so. The new hotel continued the tradition of being an important meeting place for many state legislators from outside Phoenix, so much so that the Adams was often called the "Second Capitol of Arizona." A sign on the hotel points out that its rooms are "air cooled," an important amenity for those tourists who visited in the summer months.

ABOVE: Today the Renaissance Phoenix Downtown Hotel, one of several major hotels in Phoenix's downtown, sits on the same spot. The second Hotel Adams came down in 1973 to make room for this towering structure. The 532-room hotel opened in 1975 as a Hilton, later became the Crowne Plaza Phoenix-Downtown, affiliated with Wyndham in 2003, and is now a Renaissance, a boutique hotel brand. The hotel's new owners are renovating the building and are also investing ten million dollars to make the area around the hotel more pedestrian friendly by adding shade, lighting, streetscape improvements, and spaces for special events. This action supports similar efforts throughout the downtown area. Across the street is a station for the Valley Metro Rail, or METRO, a 26-mile light rail system that began operations in 2008. The semicircular arches on the side of the hotel act as sunshades.

1931

PHOENIX TITLE AND TRUST BUILDING / ORPHEUM LOFTS

One of the last buildings of the 1920s property boom

LEFT: Here is the Phoenix Title and Trust Building, located at Adams and First Avenue, shortly after its completion in 1931. This U-shaped building had eleven stories with a steel frame and brick and terra-cotta exterior. The shape let natural light into each office. At the time it was the largest office building in the state. It is an early example of the Art Deco style in Arizona and was designed by the prolific local architectural firm of Lescher and Mahoney, which then moved its office into the building. The Title and Trust was one of the last buildings tied to the 1920s building boom. It was a symbol of prosperity and hopefulness that arrived in a time of financial trouble and despair during the Great Depression.

RIGHT: No longer an office building, the Title and Trust building now contains residential loft condominiums. The Title and Trust building continued to supply office and banking space until the late 1990s when city officials and entrepreneurs created plans to bring more residents to the downtown. With city support, the building's new owners renovated it with ninety lofts and 10,000 square feet of retail space. They gave the building the Orpheum Lofts name because of its location near the Orpheum Theatre. In 2005 its first residents moved in. The Great Recession of the late 2000s slowed the construction of new residential buildings in the downtown but since then several other condominium and apartment projects have been completed.

1921

JEFFERSON HOTEL / JEFFERSON PLACE
Featured in Alfred Hitchcock's *Psycho*

LEFT: The Jefferson Hotel, located on the southeastern corner of Central Avenue and Jefferson Street, was one of Phoenix's first upscale hotels and the area's first "high-rise" building. The Jefferson was built in 1915 by Salim Ackel, an early immigrant who owned a Phoenix clothing store, a café, a cattle ranch near Chandler, and lots of local real estate. The Jefferson had 150 rooms and half of those had private baths. The hotel was fairly popular because it was only a few blocks from the train station and close to downtown theaters and businesses. This hotel was also featured in Alfred Hitchcock's 1960 movie, *Psycho*. It is here that John Gavin and Janet Leigh carry out their affair. Hitchcock takes viewers up to the top of the building and lets them peek in the window.

ABOVE: Passenger trains no longer stop at Union Station but people will soon again be spending the night in the building. The building's new owners plan to convert the old building to condominiums and will build additional residential skyscrapers next door. This comes some thirty years after previous owners completely gutted the former hotel in 1982 and renamed it Barrister Place. They tried to entice law firms to locate offices there, an effort to capitalize on the building's close location to downtown courts, hence the name change. The plan didn't work and the City of Phoenix took over ownership of the building and used it for offices until 2010. Phoenix sold the structure to the new owners in 2016. The new owners gave a nod to the building's past by renaming it Jefferson Place.

c. 1930

LUHRS BUILDING AND LUHRS TOWER

The entire block was owned by businessman George H. N. Luhrs

LEFT: The Luhrs Building, to the left, and the Luhrs Tower are two of the most important commercial buildings in Phoenix's early history. Located southwest of Central Avenue and Jefferson Street, they are seen here in about 1930 from the nearby Luhrs Hotel. George H. N. Luhrs, a German immigrant who came to Phoenix in 1878, purchased the entire city block that both buildings now stand on and built his home. After a successful business career, Luhrs decided to promote the growth of Phoenix by building the Luhrs Building. The ten-story structure opened in 1924 and was the tallest building between El Paso, Texas, and Los Angeles. Luhrs and his son followed this by building the thirteen-story, Art Deco Luhrs Tower in 1929. The Luhrs Building was especially important to Phoenix as the home of the Arizona Club. Located at the top of the building, its members included many of the city's most important business and political leaders.

RIGHT: Both buildings are still here today, although one of the towers of the new Phoenix CityScape project sits where the Luhrs Hotel once stood. Luhrs and his son made several additions to their block, including the Luhrs U.S. Post Office Station/Arcade, a two-story annex behind the tower, and a parking garage. The Luhrs family sold the complex in 1976. Since then the buildings have had a front-row seat to the recent rebirth of Phoenix's downtown. Immediately to the east is Talking Stick Resort Area (formerly America West Area and the U.S. Airways Center), home to the NBA's Phoenix Suns, which brought new interest to the area. Development company Hansji purchased the entire block in 2007 and renamed it the Luhrs City Center, a mixed-use project with restaurants, retail space, and offices. Hansji is currently building a nineteen-story, 320-room Marriott hotel immediately to the south of the two Luhrs buildings.

c. 1925

THIRD AVENUE AND WASHINGTON STREET

The Walker Building remains, despite once being issued with a demolition permit

ABOVE: This mid-1920s photograph shows the intersection of Third Avenue and Washington Street. Toward the south, the Arizona Hotel is under construction on the other side of Washington. To the right is the Neoclassical-Revival Walker Building, built by developer J. W. Walker in 1920. Local architect L. M. Fitzhugh of the Fitzhugh and Bryan firm designed the structure, which was built of concrete and hollow tile. The building was the first Phoenix location of the J. C. Penney Company department store,

which stayed there until 1926. The Central Arizona Light and Power Company (CALPCO) then made its headquarters in the building, mounting a huge sign that lit up at night. In the 1940s, CALPCO merged with the Arizona Edison power company to become Arizona Public Service.

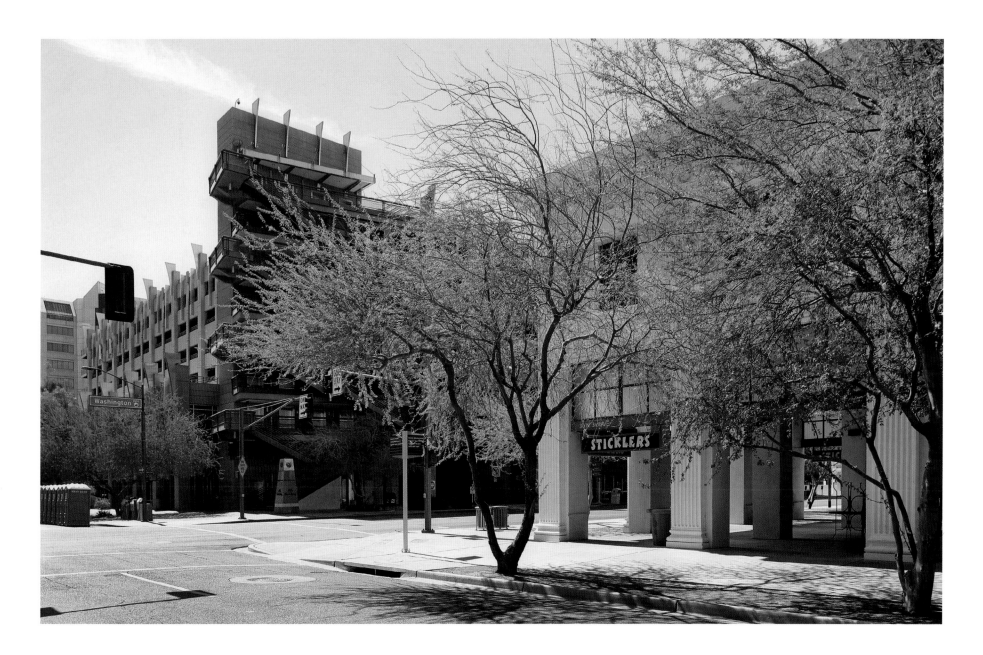

ABOVE: The Walker Building later housed a furniture company and then a labor union before the City of Phoenix purchased it in 1959 for office space. Today the Walker Building has been practically swallowed up by large Phoenix government buildings. Where the Arizona Hotel once was situated, the city-owned 305 Building now stands. The structure serves mostly as a parking garage, but city offices and some businesses occupy the ground floor. Phoenix renovated the Walker Building, which reopened in 2001, as part of the city's construction of the Phoenix Municipal Court next door. The building almost didn't make it—at one point the city even issued a demolition permit for it. Sticklers restaurant has occupied the ground floor of the Walker Building since 2004 and the American Institute of Architects has an office on the second floor.

1936

PHOENIX THEATER / MUNICIPAL COURT

The renamed and much-adapted theater was demolished in 1996

LEFT: The Phoenix Theater, shown here in 1936, was the oldest theater in Phoenix at the time. Located on Washington, between Third and Fourth avenues, it opened in 1898 as Patton's Grand Theater. Built by S. E. Patton, a theater enthusiast, the Victorian-style theater had two turrets at the top, which were later removed. As one of the largest indoor gathering places, Patton's theater was also an important site for sizeable meetings held in the city. Phoenix-area civic and agricultural leaders met here in 1900 to discuss how to build a water storage dam on the Salt River (which was later built as the Roosevelt Dam). New owners changed the theater's name to the Dorris Opera House. The Elks fraternal lodge bought it in 1908, moved into the second floor, and changed the theater's name to the Elks Theater. John Philip Sousa, the well-known composer and band leader, and his band played in this building on October 21, 1915.

RIGHT: The Phoenix Municipal Court sits on the theater's location today. Completed in 1999, it is next door to the Phoenix City Hall, which opened in 1993. The nine-story, flagstone-covered courthouse provides room for the Municipal Court, the City Prosecutor's Office, the Public Defender Eligibility Office, and part of the police department, among other offices. The city demolished the old Phoenix Theater to make way for the courthouse. At the time, the theater had a modern front and bore little resemblance to the Phoenix Theater from the 1936 view. The city also knocked down the historic A. L. Moore and Sons Mortuary, located to the north of the theater and built in 1911, to clear space for the courthouse.

ORPHEUM THEATRE

The last of the large movie palaces left in Phoenix

BELOW: The Orpheum Theatre, shown here shortly after its opening in January 1929, sits on the southwestern corner of Second Avenue and Adams Street in Phoenix. Local theater-chain owners Henry Nace, a former circus acrobat who came to Phoenix in 1910, and J. E. Rickards built the theater. They ended up with thirty-six Arizona theaters before selling out to Paramount in 1936. The noted Phoenix architectural firm of Lescher and Mahoney designed the lavish Spanish Colonial venue. It was their first commercial project and would lead to many more. At the time, the theater represented the latest innovations in entertainment. Inside visitors could admire the domed ceiling, which featured an illusionary nightfall projected by a magic-lantern machine. Called an "atmospheric-style" theater, with 1,800 seats, it staged plays, featured vaudeville, and showed movies.

1929

BELOW: The Orpheum is the last of the large theater or movie palaces left in Phoenix today—all of the others were demolished by the 1980s. The Orpheum also went through a series of owners and mistreatments that threatened its survival. At that point the Junior League of Phoenix took on the cause of saving the Orpheum. They pushed the City of Phoenix to buy the building in 1984 and backed a bond program to pay for some of its restoration. To finance the rest, Phoenix decided to build its new twenty-story City Hall, which was completed in 1993, directly behind the old theater. The theater was both modernized and extensively restored, and it reopened as a multiuse performing-arts center in 1997.

c. 1930

HOTEL SAN CARLOS

The most expensive place to stay in Phoenix when it opened

LEFT: The Hotel San Carlos around 1930. Dwight B. Heard, a wealthy real estate developer, and Charles Harris became partners and opened the seven-story Hotel San Carlos in 1928. The site, at Central and Monroe avenues, once the location of Phoenix's Central School, sat vacant for many years. Heard and Harris wanted a high-end hotel to cash in on Arizona's growing tourism industry. They hired G. Whitecross Ritchie to design the Renaissance Revival structure. Among its modern conveniences at the time were air-conditioning, steam heat, and elevators. It was the most expensive place to stay in Phoenix when it opened, but that was not a deterrent. The place quickly attracted a crowd of locals and Hollywood movie stars, including Jean Harlow, Clark Gable, Spencer Tracy, and Mae West.

ABOVE: Later owners remodeled the hotel in 1955, adding a swimming pool to the rooftop sundeck. The hotel has undergone additional renovations since then, each trying to restore the hotel's original grandeur. Those efforts paid off—the San Carlos earned the prestigious Historic Hotels of America affiliation in 1991. In 1993, its operators added the San Carlos Hollywood Star Walk on the streets around the hotel with the names of movie stars and band leaders who stayed there. The hotel still contains many of its original elements, and one of the two elevators from 1928 still operates today. The San Carlos is the only historic hotel still operating in Phoenix's downtown area, and is holding its own despite all the new hotels built recently in the area, aided by its proximity to downtown attractions and the METRO light rail system.

1935

PROFESSIONAL BUILDING

It was the place in Phoenix to go
to see a doctor or dentist

LEFT: The twelve-story Professional Building opened
at Monroe Street and Central Avenue in 1931. Here
it is in 1935. This Art Deco skyscraper was originally
designed to serve as a centralized place for medical
and dental offices, clinics, and laboratories. For
many years, it was the place in Phoenix to go to see a
doctor or dentist. The lower stories are made out of
real Indiana Limestone, while the upper stories are
stuccoed but made to look like stone. Valley National
Bank once had its offices in the building, and for a time
a 40-foot revolving sign promoting Valley National Bank
stood on top. The bank left in the early 1970s with the
completion of its new forty-story tower near Central
and Van Buren.

RIGHT: The building grew upward in 1958 with the addition of the top story. Its commercial growth hit the skids in the early 1970s when the Valley National Bank headquarters moved into the new skyscraper across the street to the north (now the Chase Tower). For many years the building sat vacant with the exception of restaurants on the ground floor. A development company purchased the structure in 2005 with the goal of turning it into a boutique hotel. It began the project by completely gutting the Professional Building in 2007. These plans were derailed by the financial crisis of the Great Recession, which slowed or canceled many construction projects in the region. The building sat vacant until 2013 when CSM Corporation purchased it for $7.9 million. With some public assistance, CSM rehabilitated the structure as a hotel. The 170-room Hilton Garden Inn opened in December 2015.

c. 1930

SECURITY BUILDING
Still at the heart of downtown's office district

LEFT: Looking south down Central Avenue near Van Buren Street around 1930, the tall structure to the right is the Security Building. This was the second of real estate developer and city booster Dwight G. Heard's major projects (the other was the Heard Building, completed in 1920). While this eight-story building was not among Phoenix's tallest, it did have the most commercial space of any building in the state at the time of its completion in 1928. This grand Renaissance Revival building has an arcaded gallery at the top floor and a corner tower. A glass-covered cupola on top of the tower contained a light beacon that could be seen for 30 miles.

RIGHT: The Security Building remains in the heart of downtown's office district, but it no longer holds the record for commercial space. A modern skyscraper, built in the 1960s, now stands between the Security Building and the San Carlos Hotel. A ninth-floor penthouse apartment was added to the Security Building in 1958 for Walter Bimson. Bimson was president of what was once Arizona's largest bank, Valley National (now Chase Bank). Maricopa County purchased the building in 2005 and completed an extensive restoration of it in 2014. Outside the building to the lower right is a station for Phoenix's new METRO light rail system. New transportation options such as this attracted new residential construction to downtown, including the apartment tower visible to the upper right of the Security Building. The thirty-four-story 44 Monroe Apartments, completed in 2008, is the tallest residential building in Phoenix.

c. 1949

MONROE STREET, BETWEEN FIRST STREET AND CENTRAL AVENUE
The department store district had disappeared by 1969

LEFT: Looking northeast from the San Carlos Hotel about 1949, the intersection of Monroe and First streets is visible. Monroe runs from the left and stretches to the tall Professional Building on the right. The edge of the department store district is visible near the center right of the view. Downtown Phoenix was a vital commercial district, attracting shoppers until the early 1950s (J. C. Penney actually built the last downtown department store in 1953). Montgomery Ward is visible, and just above it is Sears. Walking south on First Street across from Montgomery Ward, a shopper would also find the Dorris-Heyman furniture store and Goldwater's department store. This block was full of shoppers every Saturday. Just to the left of the Professional Building is the Golden West Hotel. Built in 1899 as the Steinegger Lodging House, the modern facade was added in the 1930s.

BELOW: The Hyatt Regency Hotel, completed in 1976, now takes up the block where Montgomery Ward once stood. The department stores started leaving downtown in the mid-1950s, following shoppers to the newer neighborhoods to the north, and were all gone by 1969. To the left of the Hyatt and to the right of the Chase Tower, the tallest building in Arizona, the expansion of Phoenix Civic Plaza can be seen. Begun in 1972, the plaza replaced Phoenix's skid row—a district of run-down boarding hotels known as the "Duece." During the 1970s, Phoenix started to revitalize its downtown. Lost in the center of all these tall structures is the old Golden West Hotel. It's closed now and owned by the same company that owns the Professional Building to the right. The Golden West is the earliest remaining example of a once-common lodging building downtown.

c. 1933

FIRST AVENUE, LOOKING NORTH FROM JACKSON
Warehouses clustered here because of the closeness of the railroad

LEFT: This view is looking north at downtown Phoenix about 1933. The photographer took this picture from where Jackson Street crosses over First Avenue. Phoenix's industrial and warehouse districts developed south of downtown. Warehouses clustered here because of the closeness of the railroad, which was just behind this building. The building near the upper left is the County-City Building, completed in 1929. The tall, Art Deco skyscraper in the center is the Luhrs Tower. Its older sibling, the Luhrs Building, stands to the right edge.

ABOVE: Some of the warehouses still stand on Jackson Street, although they are mostly located just to the right of this view. The County-City Building is almost entirely blocked by a parking garage and Maricopa County's Madison Street Jail. Other modern skyscrapers dwarf the two Luhrs buildings. Many of the surviving warehouses are now being used at nightclubs and restaurants, thanks to nearby sports venues. Chase Field's completion in 1998 (formerly Bank One Ballpark), the home of Major League Baseball's Arizona Diamondbacks, brought new interest to the buildings of this once remote industrial district. One of these restaurants in the revitalized Warehouse District is owned by rock star and Phoenix resident Alice Cooper. To the right, and under construction, is the Luhrs City Center Marriot, one of the city's newest skyscrapers.

c. 1930

CHAMBERS BUILDING
The Chambers Company remained here until 2000

ABOVE: The Chambers Transfer & Storage Company building at Fourth Avenue and Jackson Street was one of dozens of warehouses that grew in the area near the railroad tracks from the 1880s until World War II. Chambers was a long-established Phoenix business when it opened this new warehouse in 1923, which stored shipments that came in on the train until they could be moved by truck. Because the Chambers

Building is right next to Union Station (out of view to the right) and the traveling public, the Spanish Colonial Revival building also has stores and offices on the first floor.

ABOVE: The Chambers Building is now a telephone switching station and offices for Maricopa County government, although the first-floor retail spaces sit empty. Other former warehouses were knocked down in 1999 to make room for a new county jail, which is just across the street to the left, dashing the hopes of those who thought the "funky old" warehouses could anchor an arts district. The jail's construction set off a minor squabble between the City of Phoenix and Maricopa County, which, as a government entity, did not need to follow the zoning restrictions of another governmental entity. A public outcry got the county to promise not to destroy the Chambers Building or nearby Union Station. The Chambers Company continued to call this building home until 2000, when it moved its headquarters to Scottsdale.

PHOENIX UNION STATION
Closed to rail passenger service since 1996

BELOW: Phoenix Union Station was just a few years old when the photographer took this photograph in about 1926. These two trains belong to the Santa Fe Railroad, but it would have been possible to see a Southern Pacific train here as well—both lines used Union Station. Southern Pacific decided in 1926 to make Phoenix part of the main line and trains went directly to or from California. Opened in 1923, this Mission Revival station provided the look that tourists from the East expected, and many did come through as Phoenix's tourism industry took off in the 1920s.

c. 1926

BELOW: Don't show up at Union Station today expecting to catch a train. Amtrack—the government-sponsored provider of rail passenger service since the 1970s—stopped serving the station and Phoenix on June 2, 1996. Trains leave from Tucson or Flagstaff instead. The private railroad companies now move freight and still pass by Union Station, but their names have changed since the 1920s. Union Pacific took over the Southern Pacific in 1996. The Santa Fe merged with Burlington Northern the same year, creating Burlington Northern Santa Fe (now just BNSF). Union Station sat empty for several years, except for the occasional use by special tourist trains, but it was not forgotten by a vocal group of local railroad enthusiasts who rallied in 1999 when they thought the structure was going to be torn down. A communications company now owns the structure and houses equipment there.

c. 1930

FIRST BAPTIST CHURCH / MONROE ABBEY
The fire-ravaged building was almost demolished in 1992

LEFT: The First Baptist Church, Third Avenue and Monroe Street, about 1930. This was the congregation's third church building in Phoenix. This Spanish Colonial Revival structure, completed in 1929, sits on the site of the second church. George Merrill, an architect with the local firm of Fitzhugh and Byron, mixed a little of the Gothic Revival style from the previous church to create this distinctive house of worship. The four-story church included a rooftop garden, a seven-story bell tower, twenty-seven Bible school rooms, a 1,500-seat auditorium, and a 125-seat choir loft. It also had a small radio broadcasting studio. The church's contractor proclaimed the First Baptist Church to be "among the most complete, practical, and beautiful church buildings in the West."

ABOVE: After years of neglect and a devastating 1984 fire that left it without a roof, the former First Baptist Church building is returning to life. Like many of Phoenix's original churches, its congregation moved out of the downtown in the 1960s for a new location far to the north. The congregation actually tried to sell the building during the Great Depression when the church had trouble making its debt payments. They kept the building with the help of the local Mormon church. Vacant and dilapidated, the building was almost demolished in 1992. A non-profit group bought the old church with the aim of transforming it into affordable housing but it took twenty-two years to raise the funds. Work on the building, which will be completed in phases, began in 2014. Now called Monroe Abbey, it will be used for a variety of uses including as a special events venue.

c. 1930

HISTORIC FIRST PRESBYTERIAN CHURCH / HILLSONG PHOENIX CHURCH
The church was used by its founding community until 2012

ABOVE: The First Presbyterian Church of Phoenix, around 1930, at Fourth Avenue and Monroe. The very first Presbyterian Church in Phoenix in the 1870s was actually a brush arbor. The congregation completed its first "real" church building in 1892 at the southeast corner of Adams and Third Avenue (which was then called Papago). They stayed in the redbrick church for forty years before moving into this new building in 1927. The church community wanted their new building to be "substantial, whose beauty could endure for at least a century to come." They hired Los Angeles architect Norman Foote Marsh, who designed this Spanish Colonial Revival building. The family of developer and town booster W. J. Murphy, founder of Glendale, donated the chimes for the building.

48

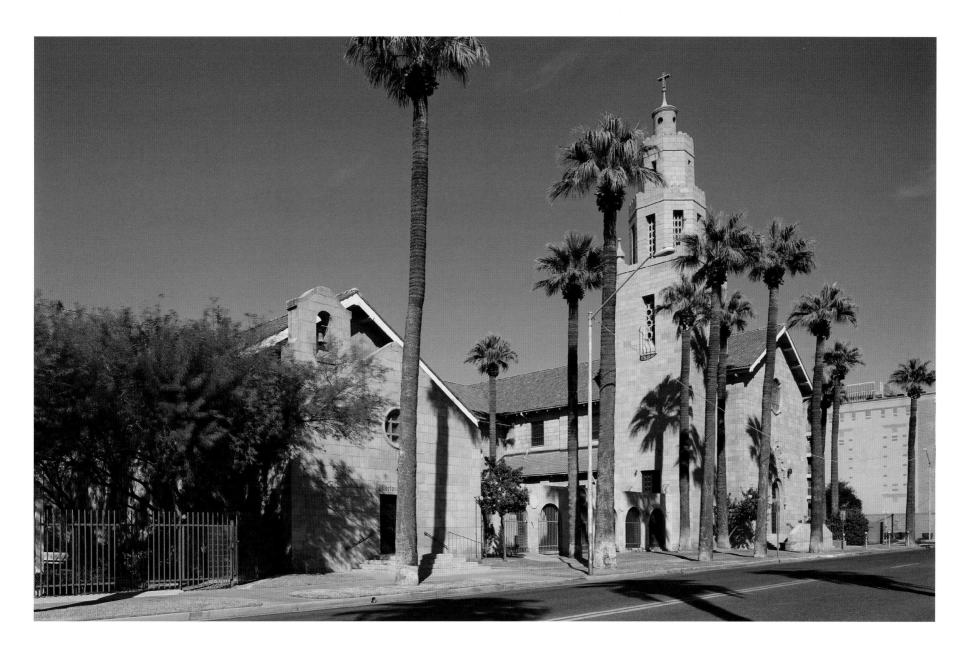

ABOVE: The beauty of the First Presbyterian Church building does indeed endure, but now as the Phoenix campus of the interdenominational Hillsong Church. Called the Historic First Church by its former congregation, it was among the last of the old Phoenix churches still used by its founding community. Many of the old downtown churches have changed hands. The First Presbyterian Church weathered many tough years. The congregation completed the church right before the Great Depression and almost lost the building in the mid-1930s, just like many other Phoenix churches at the time. Having regrouped and worked hard, they paid off the building in 1945. Many members moved out of the downtown as the Phoenix area expanded. Consequently, weekly church attendance dropped from a high of 2,800 in 1958 to less than 100 in 2012, the year the congregation sold the church. The building's new owners were attracted to the church because of its location near the Arizona State University Phoenix Campus.

c. 1930

MASONIC TEMPLE

Still home to Arizona Lodge #2

LEFT: The Phoenix Masonic Temple was built to showcase the prominence of Masons in Phoenix. F. C. Hurst designed the three-story, Neoclassical building on the southeast corner of Monroe and Fourth Avenue. It became the first permanent home for Arizona Lodge #2—originally established in October 1879—which had been meeting in various locations throughout Phoenix. It took some time to get things started, and the lodge finally purchased land in 1923. Completed in 1926, the building cost $172,000—a staggering sum at the time. Seven different Masonic lodges eventually held meetings in the new temple.

ABOVE: The Masonic Temple is still home to Arizona Lodge #2 and three other lodges. The residing lodges briefly lost control of the building during the Great Depression but were able to buy it back in 1941. By the 1990s, the structure was showing its age and needed repairs. The Masons considered selling the building and moving out. In 1996 they decided the building was a treasure to keep. As a sign of their commitment toward maintaining this historic structure, that same year the lodges applied for and received listing on the City of Phoenix's historic registry. The building underwent a major restoration between 1999 and 2001.

c. 1895

J. T. DENNIS AND MARCUS JACOBS HOMES / HERBERGER THEATER CENTER
The former Nob Hill mansions became rooming houses and slowly deteriorated

ABOVE: As the small town of Phoenix grew, its wealthy class looked for a place to build homes. As the Salt River sometimes flooded its banks and parts of Phoenix, the well-to-do selected home sites in the northeast corner of the original town site where the ground was higher. This part of town became Phoenix's Nob Hill, a name borrowed from the fancy Victorian neighborhood in San Francisco. Here are two Phoenix mansions in the 1890s, located between Second and Third streets on Monroe. The mansion to the left belonged to Marcus Jacobs. J. T. Dennis built the larger house on the right. The Queen Anne Victorian style was very popular at the time in a town that was trying to forget its desert origins.

ABOVE: The Herberger Theater Center now sits where the two mansions once stood. Nob Hill's appeal faded as downtown encroached on the neighborhood. Over time, Phoenix's wealthier citizens abandoned their neighborhoods for homes further north, especially along Central Avenue. The former Nob Hill mansions became rooming houses and slowly deteriorated. Some, like the Jacobs house, held on until the 1960s before being demolished. Built in 1989, the Herberger Center was part of Phoenix's efforts to reinvigorate a neglected downtown and to develop the local arts scene. This performing-arts venue, home to two theater companies and the occasional host to several others, is named for Robert and Katherine Herberger, who have supported many Phoenix-area arts organizations. The center went through a $16 million renovation and update in 2010.

c. 1920

SAINT MARY'S CATHOLIC BASILICA
The oldest Catholic parish in the Phoenix area

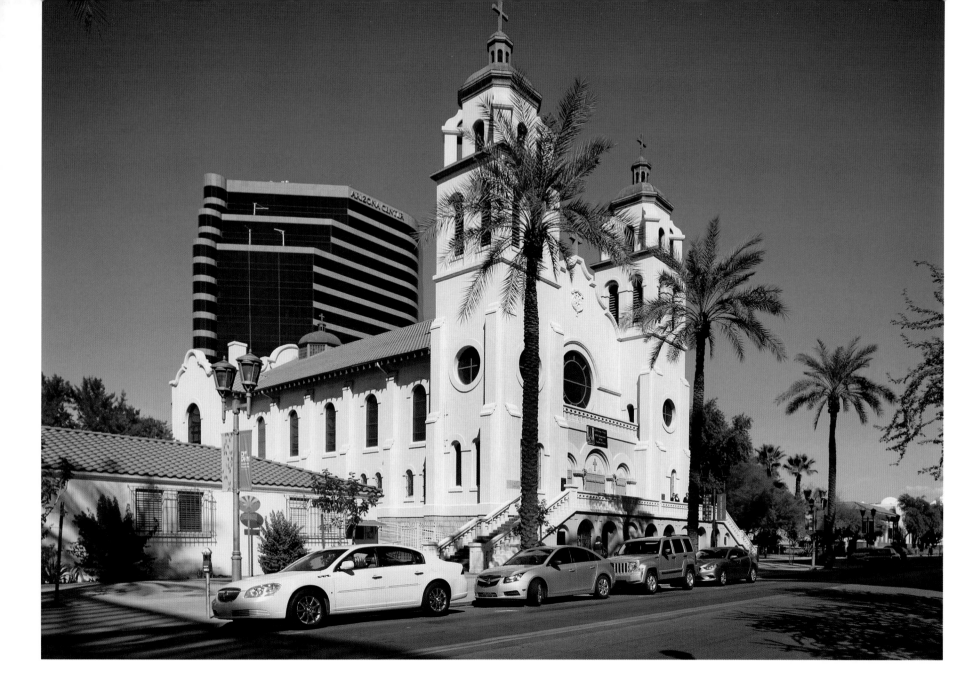

LEFT: St. Mary's Catholic Church, located near the northeast corner of Third Street and Monroe, sits on the site of Phoenix's first Catholic church, a small adobe structure built in 1881 and torn down in 1902 to make way for the new one. St. Mary's is the oldest Catholic presence in the Phoenix area, and the church has been staffed through most of its history by Franciscan priests. The church complex also included St. Mary's elementary school. Officials dedicated this Mission Revival church, designed by R. A. Gray and George Gallagher, in 1915. The completed church featured beautiful stained-glass windows created by the Munich School of Stained Glass Art.

ABOVE: Since 1989, the church has been overwhelmed by new development in the downtown. The Arizona Center shopping complex stands to the north and Chase Field, home to Major League Baseball's Arizona Diamondbacks, to the south. The church will be further obscured by a seven-story addition to the Phoenix Civic Plaza, a convention center, just to the southwest. The Diocese of Phoenix has also changed the area, tearing down the parish's elementary school behind the church and replacing it with a new diocesan headquarters. In 1985, Pope John Paul II designated St. Mary's a minor basilica in honor of its contribution to the history of the region. He visited Phoenix and St. Mary's in September 1987.

c. 1920

ROSSON HOUSE

The crowning jewel of the Heritage Square historic district

LEFT: Dr. Roland Lee Rosson came to Arizona as an army surgeon at Camp McDowell. He married Flora B. Murray, member of a wealthy local family, and opened his own medical practice in Phoenix. Flora purchased an entire city block in the original Phoenix town site for $1,000, and, in 1895, on three of the lots, the Rossons hired local architect Alexander P. Petit to build them an Eastlake house. Petit moved his practice from San Francisco and introduced the use of brick for construction to Phoenix, where builders were accustomed to using adobe. The Rossons did not live in the house very long before they rented it to Whitlaw Reid, editor of the *New York Tribune* and future U.S. ambassador to Britain. Reid came out to Arizona because he hoped the dry air would ease his asthma.

RIGHT: The house is now a museum that looks much the way it did when the Rossons first moved in. The couple sold the house in 1897 and moved to California, where Dr. Rosson died the following year. The house had many owners over the next seventy-five years or so, as many of the more wealthy residents left the downtown area and moved north. The Rosson's old home was a rooming house when the City of Phoenix bought it and the other structures on the block in 1974. Known as Block 14, it housed the last remaining houses in the original Phoenix town site. Phoenix restored the Rosson House as a museum and the centerpiece of the Heritage Square historic district. Restaurants and stores are in the other buildings.

c. 1902

BOUVIER-TEETER HOUSE

Now home to a Japanese restaurant

LEFT: Leon Bouvier, a cattleman and flour mill operator, built this house in 1899. Bouvier only lived here a short time before he rented it out. This is how the house appeared around 1902, based on the curved-dash car, the car's wooden spokes, and the family's clothing. This bungalow-style house is located on Adams Street, on the southern end of Block 14 of the original Phoenix town site. Edward Haustgen, an immigrant from Luxembourg, bought the house in 1911. His family owned a lot of real estate in the Phoenix area, and he later bought the Stevens house next door, to the west. One of the longtime residents of this house was Eliza Teeter from Tempe. She moved into the house in 1919.

ABOVE: The house is now part of Phoenix's Heritage Square, an area of restored historic houses and museums in downtown Phoenix. The square sits just across the street to the east of Phoenix Civic Plaza convention center. Completed in 1972, Civic Plaza was the anchor of Phoenix's plans to revitalize the old downtown. Phoenix cleared a couple blocks of old houses and cheap hotels to make way for Civic Plaza and the adjacent Phoenix Symphony Hall. These projects left Block 14 as the only remaining cluster of original homes from the old Phoenix town site. Then-mayor John Driggs proposed saving and transforming the block into Heritage Square. Today the Bouvier-Teeter Building is an Asian-style tea house and Japanese restaurant called Nobuo at Teeter House.

PHOENIX UNION HIGH SCHOOL
The only high school in Phoenix for many years

c. 1917

LEFT: Phoenix Union High School, shown here around 1917, had a sprawling campus on the northwest corner of Seventh Street and Van Buren. The students are coming down the steps of the Domestic Arts and Sciences Building. Next door is the auditorium, and across the plaza is the Sciences Building. These three buildings were constructed between 1911 and 1912. The idea that several buildings could be used as a high school campus was a novelty. The other two contemporary examples of this concept in the Southwest were in California. Los Angeles architect Norman Foote Marsh designed all three. The campus, particularly the auditorium, which was entirely rebuilt in 1929, was the site of many cultural and social activities in Phoenix. This was the only high school in Phoenix for many years, and at its peak in the 1930s, the campus had eleven buildings and over 5,000 students.

BELOW: These are the only buildings that remain on the former campus after the last students left in 1982. Now these buildings anchor the 30-acre Phoenix Biomedical Campus (PBC). Focused on bioscience and healthcare, the center's partners search for cures for various chronic and deadly diseases. It started in 2002 when the city convinced Dr. Jeffrey Trent, one of the scientists who led a successful effort to map the human genome, to move to Phoenix. Trent's Translational Genomics Research Institute (TGen) occupies one of several new structures built for the center. As for the high school buildings, the first two—the former Domestic Arts and Sciences building and the auditorium—are used by the University of Arizona College of Medicine-Phoenix, which accepted its first students in 2007. The University of Arizona College of Pharmacy occupies the Sciences building. A 2014 study determined that the regional economic impact of both the biomedical complex and the medical school was over $2 billion.

1916

MONROE SCHOOL / THE CHILDREN'S MUSEUM OF PHOENIX

The former Monroe School is still a place for children to learn and play

LEFT: The student body of Monroe School posed for this photograph in front of their school in January 1916. The school opened near the heart of downtown Phoenix, near Seventh Street and Van Buren, in 1914. It was within walking distance of the Phoenix Union High School. Designed by Los Angeles architect Norman Foote Marsh, this was the first school in Phoenix to choose a design that was something other than a Victorian style. Students entered this three-story, Neoclassical Revival school through an imposing portal of columns, which evoked the importance of education in the capital of a young state. Monroe School was the largest and grandest elementary school in the region, and it served students from a variety of social backgrounds. Although it was in the middle of the city, the school was surrounded by a large playground.

ABOVE: Children once again play and learn in the former Monroe School building. The Children's Museum of Phoenix opened in 2008 after a major renovation. The museum offers over 300 interactive areas for children up to age ten. Started in 1998 by parents in central Phoenix and originally called the Phoenix Family Museum, it found support from the City of Phoenix. The win-win partnership gave the museum a building and gave Phoenix a tenant for one of its most threatened historic buildings. The Monroe School closed in 1972 as much of the school-aged population moved away from the city-center. The federal government later purchased and renovated the building, using it for a military recruiting station. After the recruiting station moved out in 1998, the building sat vacant while new construction, including nearby Chase Field, abounded downtown. Worried about losing the school to demolition, Phoenix bought it in 2002 using funds approved by voters. Over 300,000 people visited the museum in 2015.

1937

HOTEL WESTWARD HO
A well-known Phoenix landmark

LEFT: In this picture taken of Central Avenue in 1937, two important Phoenix buildings are visible. The smaller one to the left is the Phoenix Post Office. Opened in 1935, the federal government originally wanted the structure to have seven floors to house government offices. The Great Depression both delayed the building and forced the project to be scaled back significantly to only two floors. The towering building across the street is the Hotel Westward Ho. This sixteen-story building opened in 1929 and became one of the Phoenix area's most recognized landmarks. Its ballroom was a popular place for dances in the 1930s and during World War II, and the Thunderbird Dinner Theater was a great place for a date. The hotel also attracted the famous. Roy Rogers once got his horse Trigger to climb the stairs in the lobby. Elizabeth Taylor rented a suite on a year-round basis. The hotel also made an appearance in Marilyn Monroe's 1956 movie, *Bus Stop*.

RIGHT: Both buildings are still there today. The Westward Ho, one of only two of Phoenix's major historic hotel buildings to survive (the San Carlos is the other) became subsidized housing for the elderly in 1981. A radio antenna now sits on top. A group called the Phoenix Preservation Partnership bought the structure in 2003 and restored it in 2004. The theater and other spaces have been converted to apartments. The new owners painted the tower gray after learning that the color had graced the Westward Ho when it first opened. The Arizona State University Downtown Phoenix Campus, established in 2006, is located to the right of the photograph. ASU's Center for Applied Behavior Health Policy is now located on the ground floor of the Westward Ho. As for the post office, it became the campus's student center in 2013. The growth of the campus has been aided by the METRO light rail, which runs down the center of Central Avenue.

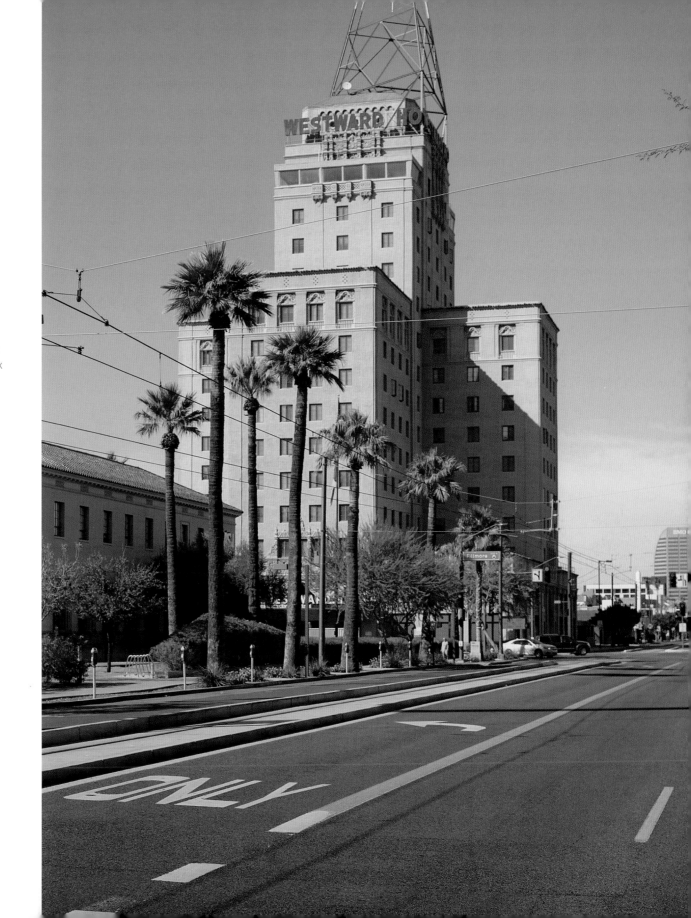

CARNEGIE LIBRARY
The city's first free public library

BELOW: Shown here around 1930, the Phoenix Carnegie Library sits on a long block between Washington and Jefferson streets and Tenth and Twelfth avenues. This was the city's first free public library, and its construction was the result of ten years of effort by a group of volunteers who thought the young city needed such a place. The library is named for Andrew Carnegie, the wealthy businessman who helped build libraries throughout the United States. He donated $25,000 for the construction of this building and the City of Phoenix donated the land. Designed by local architect W. R. Norton, with a few changes made at the City Council's request, the library opened in 1907. The library's grounds were also part of a city park that served the surrounding neighborhood between downtown Phoenix to the east and the State Capitol grounds to the west.

c. 1930

BELOW: Today the Arizona Department of Libraries, Archives, and Public Records operates the building as the Carnegie Center, which offers a variety of electronic library resources and services. Phoenix kept the old Carnegie Library open until 1952, when the Phoenix Public Library moved to a new location at Central and McDowell Road. Following the move, the old library became an adult recreation center, a clothing distribution center, a reading room, and a warehouse. Meanwhile the surrounding neighborhood declined, many houses were demolished, and the library park became a refuge for the homeless. The State of Arizona took over the site in the mid-1980s, restored the library, and opened a museum within it. Since then, new government building projects are filling in the former neighborhoods between downtown Phoenix and the State Capitol.

c. 1920

ARIZONA CAPITOL

The Capitol Building ensured that Phoenix kept the capital for good

ABOVE: The Arizona State Capitol Building, at Seventeenth Avenue and Washington, about 1920. During its first thirty years, the Territory of Arizona had a "capital on wheels." The capital swung between the Arizona towns of Prescott and Tucson before Phoenix captured the prize in 1889. Constructed between 1898 and 1900, this capitol building ensured that Phoenix kept the capital for good. Phoenix remained the capital when Arizona became a state in 1912. James Riely Gordon won the national design competition by entering his rejected plan for the capitol building of Mississippi. Cash-strapped Arizona officials reduced the scale and cost of Gordon's design by eliminating a grand staircase to a planned second-floor entrance. They also passed on the suggestion to make the capitol dome from copper to recognize Arizona's dominant copper industry. They painted the dome copper instead.

ABOVE: As the population of Arizona exploded during the post–World War II boom, so did the size of Arizona's government, and it quickly outgrew Gordon's building. Rejecting a fantastic proposal by famed architect Frank Lloyd Wright, Arizona instead built separate modern-looking buildings for the senate and house of representatives in 1956. In 1974, the governor moved into a new "executive tower" skyscraper right behind the capitol building. Having lost its original government function, Arizona transformed the old capitol building into a museum in 1981 following a restoration that put real copper on the building's dome. The restoration also freed the "Winged Victory" weather vane that legislators in the 1950s had fixed in place so that her back would never face them.

c. 1957

AERIAL VIEW OF DOWNTOWN PHOENIX, LOOKING NORTHEAST
All of the skyscrapers in this 1950s view were built or started during the prosperous 1920s

LEFT: This view, looking northeast, shows Phoenix's industrial district, centered on Union Station in the middle. Beyond the central business district are many of Phoenix's residential neighborhoods. Open space separates Phoenix from the mountains on the horizon, such as the McDowells to the far right. Prominently featured at the top left is one of Phoenix's notable mountains, Squaw Peak. All of the skyscrapers seen in this view were built or started during the prosperous times of the 1920s. Commercial building largely came to a halt during the Great Depression, and in a sense, the downtown was "frozen" until after World War II.

ABOVE: Downtown "thawed" in the 1950s and the skyline shows buildings from every decade since then, including several built in just the last few years. Union Station is visible to the south of downtown. The big rectangular building to the far left, with the solar panels on it, is the Sandra Day O'Connor Federal Courthouse, completed in 2002 and named for the first woman on the U.S. Supreme Court. To the middle left is the Westward Ho, once a hotel. In the upper left is the former Squaw Peak, a name considered offensive by many. The state renamed it Piestewa Peak in 2003. Private Lori Piestewa, a member of the Hopi tribe in northeastern Arizona, died in the war in Iraq in 2003. She was the first Native American woman in the U.S. armed forces to die in combat.

c. 1925

KENILWORTH SCHOOL
The oldest public school still operating in Maricopa County

LEFT: The Kenilworth School, on north Fifth Avenue, was completed in 1920. The imposing Neoclassical building, designed by Norman Foote Marsh, was one of the first schools built outside of Phoenix's original town site. Phoenix had a population of 29,000 in 1920 and was starting to expand north from the historic town center. More schools were needed, and the district built Kenilworth Elementary to meet the demand. Because it was built on the north side of Phoenix, the school catered to some of the city's more prominent families. Arizona Senator Barry Goldwater graduated from here, as did Arizona governor and senator Paul Fannin. Margaret T. Hance, a former mayor of Phoenix, also went to the school. Today a park nearby bears her name.

ABOVE: Kenilworth is still a school today, although its surrounding neighborhood was demolished to make room for the Interstate 10 freeway, or Inner Loop. The freeway is within sight of the school to the south, but transportation planners changed the freeway alignment slightly in the 1980s to save this historic structure. With 650 students today, this public school is the oldest still operating in Maricopa County. Kenilworth's Montessori program also attracts students from around the valley and has a waiting list. The district rehabilitated the structure in the early 1980s and added a new annex in the 1990s. The school celebrated its eightieth anniversary in 2000 by restoring one of the classrooms to the way it looked in the 1920s.

THE ELLIS-SHACKELFORD HOUSE

The only intact mansion left along the downtown section of Central Avenue

BELOW: Dr. William C. Ellis's house, on north Central Avenue, about 1920. Moving to Phoenix from Ohio in 1907, Ellis helped organize the Arizona Deaconess Hospital (now the Good Samaritan Medical Center) and was the head of its medical staff. From the 1890s to the 1930s, Central Avenue's rural feel attracted many of the Phoenix wealthy who wanted to live in the country and yet be close to the city. Their large homes lined the sides of Central Avenue, earning the neighborhood the nickname of "Millionaires' Row." Local architect R. A. Gray designed the house at a time when the Craftsman Bungalow style was very popular in Arizona, and the house is a blend of the Prairie and Bungalow styles. Completed in 1917, the house featured three stories, a basement, hardwood floors, mahogany trim and banisters, hand-painted globe-style chandeliers, and wire-cut bricks from Colorado.

c. 1920

BELOW: Today the house is the only intact mansion left along the downtown section of Central Avenue. The house now sits on the north side of the Interstate 10 or Papago freeway, which cuts right through the center of Phoenix. The Phoenix Burton Barr Central Library, with its desert climate-sensitive design by William Bruder, sits across the street. Dr. Ellis's daughter and her husband, J. Gordon Shackleford, inherited the house and lived there until 1964. The house was used as a boys' home and a museum of the Arizona Historical Society. The Arizona Department of Transportation acquired the house during the construction of the freeway and later sold it to the City of Phoenix. The city completed a major restoration of the house in 2013 and shares the building with Arizona Humanities for office and meeting space.

c. 1930

TEMPLE BETH ISRAEL BUILDING / CUTLER-PLOTKIN JEWISH HERITAGE CENTER

The building is once again a meeting place for Phoenix's Jewish community

ABOVE: Phoenix had 29,000 people in 1920 and had just become Arizona's largest city when Temple Beth Israel, a Reform congregation, organized. Jewish Americans started arriving in Phoenix in the 1870s, but it took a while until this community could support a synagogue. This congregation built the first synagogue in Phoenix around 1921. Several prominent local businessmen, including Isaac Diamond, David Goldberg, and

David Grunow, helped lead the effort. Located at 122 East Culver, a few blocks south of McDowell Road, the building was a place of worship, a community center, and a gathering place. Here is the synagogue complex in about 1930. The building to the left was a classroom, completed in 1924. The synagogue, just a few blocks east of Central Avenue, was centrally located for Phoenix's Jewish community.

ABOVE: Today the building is the Cutler-Plotkin Jewish Heritage Center. The building had not been associated with the Phoenix Jewish community for nearly fifty years before that though. Following World War II, Phoenix started to grow north and many Jewish Americans moved out of the downtown area. Temple Beth Israel relocated in 1949 to better serve its congregation. The Chinese Baptist Church purchased the building and called it home until 1959. Because of the Phoenix area's growing Hispanic population, the former synagogue eventually became the Iglesia Bautista, a Mexican-language Baptist church. It sold the building to the Arizona Jewish Historical Society in 2003, which restored and transformed the building into a museum, educational center, and event venue. Named for Rabbi Emeritus Albert Plotkin and donor Lawrence Cutler, the Jewish Heritage Center opened in 2010.

c. 1920

NORTON HOUSE

Dr. James C. Norton was responsible for keeping Arizona's cattle herds healthy

LEFT: The Norton House, shown here in about 1920, was, at the time, north of Phoenix, located on Fifteenth Avenue between McDowell and Thomas roads. Dr. James C. Norton was a veterinarian and former Iowa college professor who moved to Arizona for health reasons. In 1893 he became the territorial veterinarian and was responsible for keeping Arizona's cattle herds healthy. He left that job in 1912, bought 200 acres in the country, and started a dairy farm. Dr. Norton also founded a local YMCA and was active in the First Presbyterian Church of Phoenix. He had this Renaissance Revival house built and moved his family into it in 1913. The house had two sleeping porches along the back of the house for keeping cool during warmer weather. The family loved to play croquet on the large lawn in the front.

ABOVE: The Phoenix Parks and Recreation Department maintains its headquarters in the house, as it has since 1935. The screened sleeping porch has been filled in and the rooms have been converted into offices. The City of Phoenix bought the house from Dr. Norton, along with half of Norton's 200-acre property, in the early 1930s. Phoenix then launched an ambitious program to develop new parks. The city transformed its portion of Norton's land into Encanto Park, which included a lagoon, boathouse, and golf course. Norton, who lived until 1954, developed the rest of his property as the Del Norte Estates neighborhood.

c. 1912

PHOENIX INDIAN SCHOOL

Originally part of the federal government's plan to assimilate Native Americans

ABOVE: Seen here about 1912, the Dining Hall stands behind the lagoon on the 160-acre campus of the Phoenix Indian School. Built as an auditorium in 1901, school officials transformed the building into a dining hall in 1903 to meet the needs of the growing school. The Phoenix Indian School opened to the northeast of Phoenix in 1891. Indian School Road runs along the school's southern boundary. The school, one in a national system of schools, was part of the federal government's plan to assimilate Native Americans by teaching English and manual and domestic labor skills. The government forcibly took Native American children from their parents, cut their hair, put them in military uniforms, and punished them for speaking native languages. The campus also included an auditorium, dormitories, a band field, a farm, and related buildings.

ABOVE AND LEFT: The Dining Hall is one of only three buildings from the Indian School, as well as the oldest of the three, that remains today after the campus closed in 1990. A federal policy change emphasizing reservation schools over boarding schools eventually led to the closing of this ninety-nine-year-old institution. The federal government, which owned the school, divided the 160-acre property three ways in the mid-1990s: it traded the valuable Central Avenue portion to a developer, gave some of it to the Carl T. Hayden Veterans Administration Medical Center on the east end of the property, and let the City of Phoenix have the middle portion. The developer still has not started on its share of the land, and the future of this parcel is unknown, but the city has. Phoenix transformed its section into a park, complete with a lake where the lagoon once was, and restored the three surviving school buildings. Steele Indian School Park opened in 2001 and has become a popular recreational destination.

1931

GRUNOW CLINIC
One of the city's most distinctive entrances

LEFT: Shown here in 1931, the Grunow Memorial Clinic, at 926 E. McDowell Road, was named for Lois Anita Grunow, who died in 1929 when she was seven. Her parents, owners of a successful manufacturing company, donated the money to build the clinic. Designed by L. M. Fitzhugh and Lester Byron, this Spanish Colonial Revival building has one of the more distinctive entrances in Phoenix. The entrance facade and building windows have Churrigueresque detailing (elaborate stone carvings). Inside the entrance, in the Renaissance room, are murals of early physicians painted by local Lon Megargee, who later gained some fame as a cowboy artist. This medical office is right across the street from the Good Samaritan Hospital, one of the largest hospitals in the Phoenix area at the time. The hospital opened here in 1923 and attracted other medical businesses and buildings to the area.

RIGHT: The Grunow Clinic still stands on McDowell Road and the building is still used for medical offices. Most Phoenix-area residents know about the Grunow Clinic from one of Arizona's most spectacular and grisly murders. Winnie Ruth Judd, dubbed the "trunk murderess" by the press, worked as a secretary in the building. Judd was accused of killing her two roommates in 1931, dismembering the bodies, and shipping them in trunks to Los Angeles. The Hearst newspapers in California sensationalized the case, and Judd was convicted and spent much of her life in the Arizona State Hospital. Most Phoenix residents thought she took the blame for a crime committed by a prominent businessman, who they believed was protected by the Phoenix business establishment. Across the street, the original Good Samaritan building has been replaced by a large, modern hospital.

c. 1900

OSBORN SCHOOL / OSBORN ROAD AND CENTRAL AVENUE

The school was demolished in 1963 to make way for the Financial Center

LEFT: Seen here in about 1900, the Osborn School was a rural school located far to the north of Phoenix on Central Avenue and what is today the northeast corner of Central and Osborn Road. It was established in the early 1880s, and the original two-story building was completed in 1892. James A. Creighton was the architect, and he gained a prominent reputation for designing this school and numerous other buildings in the Phoenix area in the 1880s and 1890s. His best-known structure today is Old Main on the campus of the University of Arizona in Tucson. Osborn School was named for one of the school's founding board members, John P. Osborn.

ABOVE AND RIGHT: The corner is now host to the Financial Center, designed by St. Louis architect W. A. Sarmiento and built around 1965. This intersection lies in the heart of the Uptown district of Central Avenue. Uptown is generally that portion of Central north of McDowell Road. Many Phoenix offices started to leave the downtown for this area in the 1950s, paralleling the departure of private homes and retail businesses. Occupying what had become valuable real estate, the Osborn School closed down and was demolished in 1963. In the years prior to the school's destruction, the school district made several changes to the historic structure, including flattening the roof and expanding the campus.

CENTRAL AVENUE DAIRY / PARK CENTRAL MALL

The dairy gave way to Phoenix's first mall

BELOW: In 1937, the Central Avenue Dairy was located north of town in the country. The dairy was about a mile north of some of the fancier homes south of McDowell Road and Central Avenue. The population of Phoenix totaled about 60,000 people at the time. This building was located near the present-day alignment of Earl Drive, and on the west side of Central Avenue. This photograph shows the dependable form of transportation that delivery drivers relied on each morning as they traveled to points throughout Phoenix. The large dairy, owned by the Geare family, remained in operation right up until the early 1950s.

1937

BELOW: The site of the old dairy is now part of a sprawling, mixed-use office center called Park Central. Park Central was once an open-air shopping mall, the first mall in Phoenix, opened in 1957. The mall was closer to Phoenix's new suburban neighborhoods. This same trend led to the mall's demise in the early 1990s. The city kept moving north and new malls opened. Dillard's department store, the last of the major tenants, closed in 1995. New owners transformed the mall into office space. Taking advantage of Park Central's location near St. Joseph's Hospital, several health care businesses moved in. Park Central still includes a few small businesses and restaurants that cater to the office workers from the nearby section of Central Avenue known as Uptown. The classic cars in this photo are taking part in Arizona's biannual Cruise on Central car show.

1928

BROPHY COLLEGE PREPARATORY SCHOOL
Urban Phoenix now surrounds the once-isolated college campus

LEFT: This photograph from 1928 shows Brophy College Preparatory School with Camelback Mountain in the background. Ellen Amelia Goodbody Brophy established this Catholic school in honor of her late husband, William Henry Brophy. The Jesuits, a religious order, operated the school. The Spanish Colonial Regis Hall, which contained a chapel and the Jesuits' residence, sits just east of Central Avenue on 19 acres that were once part of the Brophy estate. Part of the meandering Arizona Canal is to the right. The chapel also served as St. Francis Xavier Parish, the second Catholic parish in Phoenix. Ellen came to Arizona in the 1890s with her husband, a successful mining company executive and banker. A devoted Catholic, she helped establish several churches and schools. Pope Pius XI honored Mrs. Brophy for her work in 1931. She died in 1934.

ABOVE: Phoenix has grown and filled in the space between Camelback Mountain at the top and Central Avenue at the bottom. On the left, Camelback Road stretches east toward the mountain. The cluster of tall buildings just below the mountain is the Biltmore area, centered on Twenty-fourth Street and Camelback. The area is named for the Biltmore Resort and its surrounding neighborhoods to the left. Developers also built new office and apartment buildings along Central Avenue before the METRO light rail opened in 2008. Trains pass by Brophy College Preparatory School and the Phoenix Central High School across the canal to the right. Brophy struggled through hard economic times after opening and closed in 1935. The all-male high school reopened in 1952. It added several buildings to its once-rural site, including the Spanish Revival Saint Francis Xavier Church (1959). Several structures have been completed since the 2000s. About 1,200 students now attend the nationally recognized school.

c. 1935

WRIGLEY MANSION

Built as a winter cottage for the founder of the famous chewing gum company

ABOVE: William Wrigley Jr., who made his fortune selling chewing gum, built the Wrigley Mansion as a fiftieth wedding anniversary gift for his wife, Ada. Constructed between 1929 and 1931, it was the largest private residence in the state at the time. Here it is in the 1930s. The 17,000-square-foot house had twenty-four bedrooms, twelve bathrooms, and eleven fireplaces, yet the Wrigleys only used it as a winter cottage during their four-to-eight-week visits from Chicago each year. The house was one of five that they owned. Los Angeles architect Earl Heitschmidt included elements of the California Monterey, Mediterranean, and Spanish Colonial Revival styles in the design of the mansion, which the Wrigleys called La Colina Solana, or "the Sunny Hill." At the time, there were no other buildings within 10 miles of the mansion.

ABOVE: William Wrigley Jr. passed away in 1932 and Ada died in 1958. The Wrigley family, which also purchased the nearby Arizona Biltmore Resort, continued to own the mansion for many years. They had the house included in the zoning for the resort in the 1960s. In 1973, the family sold the mansion, the resort, and an adjacent golf course to Tally Industries. Tally used the mansion as a public function facility and as an extra guest lodge for the hotel. Western Savings purchased the mansion in 1979 and turned it into the Mansion Club, a private club and corporate resort. Interested in preserving the landmark mansion, the late George "Geordie" Hormel—musician, recording studio proprietor, and heir to the meatpacking family—purchased the house in 1992 along with his wife Jamie. They restored the house and grounds to their 1930s appearance, and the complex is now available for corporate meetings, weddings, and other events.

c. 1940

ARIZONA BILTMORE

Often assumed to be a Frank Lloyd Wright design

LEFT: Brothers Charles and Warren McArthur were operating a Dodge dealership in Phoenix when they got a brainstorm to build a resort. Having escaped their hometown Chicago winters, they thought that Arizona would make a popular destination when the rest of the country was snowed in. Their idea blossomed into the Arizona Biltmore, shown here about 1940. At the time the resort was located about 8 miles to the northeast of Phoenix, on the bank of the Arizona Canal. The McArthurs' older brother, Albert, a commercial architect who once worked for famed architect Frank Lloyd Wright, designed the building. In developing the hotel's distinctive "Biltmore Block," Albert consulted with Wright about using a type of cast–concrete block technique, which Albert mistakenly thought Wright had developed. The Prairie-style hotel opened on February 23, 1929.

ABOVE: The resort now sits in the middle of the prestigious Biltmore neighborhood in Phoenix, northeast of Camelback Road and Twenty-fourth Street. The original hotel and complex of fifteen cottages has since expanded to include a conference center, seven tennis courts, eight swimming pools, several restaurants and stores, and condominiums. The hotel continues to attract a high-end clientele, including every president from Herbert Hoover to George W. Bush. Unfortunately the McArthurs did not share in its success. Charles and Warren lost the resort to chewing gum entrepreneur William Wrigley Jr. following the 1929 stock market crash. Albert lost credit for designing the resort after a 1973 fire severely damaged the hotel; the owners at the time turned to Wright's Taliesin West architectural school to repair the damage, which led to the common misconception that Wright designed the resort.

TOVREA CASTLE AT CARRARO HEIGHTS

This wedding-cake-style house was built to resemble a medieval Italian castle

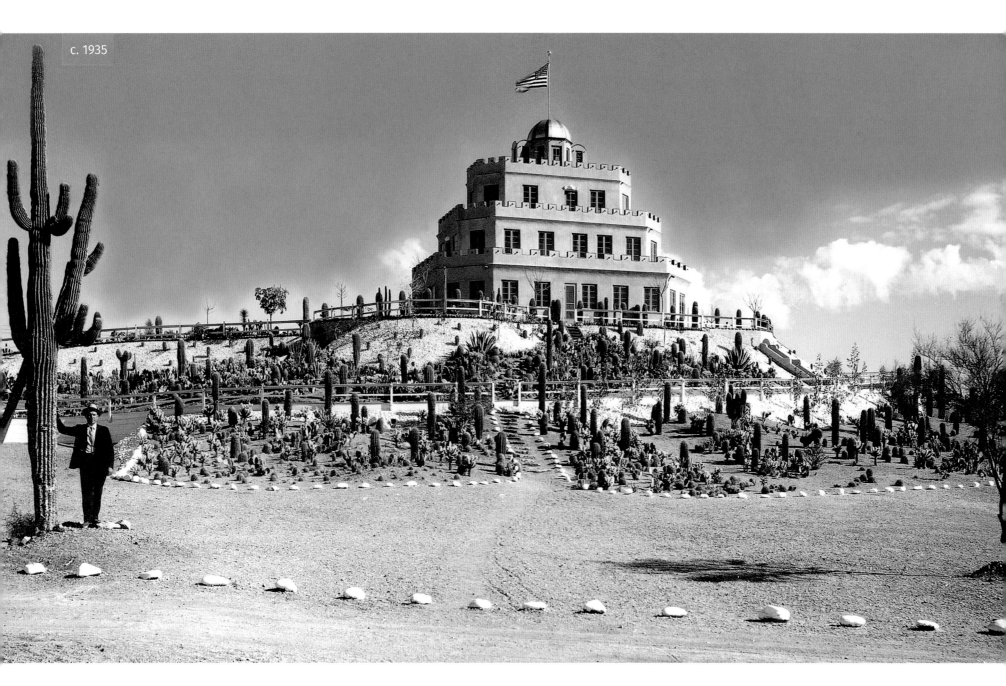

c. 1935

LEFT: Alessio Carraro finished building this wedding-cake-style house in 1930. Carraro was an Italian immigrant who found financial success with a San Francisco sheet-metal business. He wanted to use this house as a hotel and the centerpiece for Carraro Heights, an upscale residential development he planned to build. Carraro based the design on his vision of a medieval Italian castle and built the house himself with the help of his son and some hired laborers. M. Moktatchev, a traveling Russian author and gardener, landscaped the grounds with hundreds of species of cacti from around the world. The project was finished in late 1930, and Carraro celebrated by outlining the building with hundreds of painted lightbulbs.

BELOW: Tovrea Castle at Carraro Heights, as it is now known, is no longer remote and can easily be seen from nearby 202 freeway. Carraro's plan for his plush resort crashed when Edward Tovrea bought land nearby for a slaughterhouse and sheep pens. Realizing that no one would want to build a fancy house next to sheep, Carraro sold the property to an anonymous buyer. That buyer was Della Tovrea, Edward's wife. Edward died and Della eventually married William Plato Stuart. The couple wintered in the house until Stuart died in 1960. Burglars robbed the house in 1969, injuring Della, and she later died from her injuries. Unoccupied from then, it suffered from neglect and many of the cacti died. The City of Phoenix bought the house in 1993. The city and a non-profit group completed a restoration of the house and opened it for tours in 2012. The cactus garden surrounding the house was also restored.

1940

COTTAGE COURT

The old motor hotels were bypassed by the new interstate highways

ABOVE: Cottage Court was a Phoenix "motor court" or early motel, at 5218 East Van Buren Road. Auto tourism began in the early twentieth century as automobile ownership became widespread and employers offered vacation time. Hotels were often too formal and expensive so travelers would camp wherever they ended their day. Towns across the nation followed by setting up free "auto camps." The nation developed interconnected roads and adopted a uniform system for designating highways in 1925. Van Buren became part of three transcontinental highways

(including U.S. 60) in the 1930s. When towns started charging fees for crowded camps, the auto camping business was born. As the term "camp" wasn't upscale enough for these new businesses, they called themselves lodges, cabins, cottages, and courts. These places developed a common layout with individual cabins centered on a courtyard but competed with different themes. The travel industry boomed after World War II.

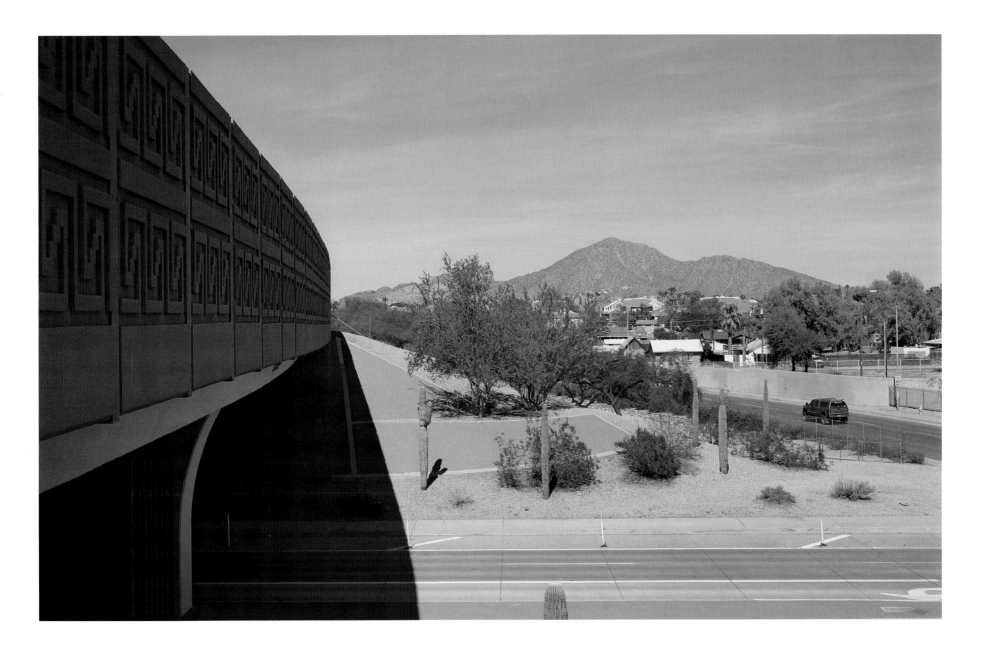

ABOVE: The former Cottage Court is long gone, left behind by changes in the lodging industry and bypassed by the new interstate highways. The Cottage Court changed owners and names as the industry changed. Motor courts evolved into motels with more services. National brands developed which promised travelers the same level of services wherever they were. Corporate and franchised owners of these brands began to put the local motels out of business. At the same time the modern Interstate Highway System developed and bypassed the original highways. The Van Buren motel industry was devastated. In 1962, forty-two of sixty-one Phoenix hotels were located on Van Buren but this dropped to thirty-two out of sixty-three in 1969. The final blow to Van Buren came in 1989 when it lost its last highway designation, as Highway 60, to the recently completed Papago Freeway (I-10) through central Phoenix. The Interstate 10 did not even have an exchange with Van Buren.

c. 1930

PAPAGO PARK

Urban growth has made this hilly desert park more accessible to visitors

LEFT: The red-hued Papago Buttes are probably the most stunning land feature in the region, aside from Camelback Mountain. Early on, the Buttes became a popular place for picnicking and horseback riding, as shown in this photograph from around 1930. Just out of view is the Buttes' most-recognized feature, Hole-in-the-Rock. The beauty of the area and threats from population growth led the federal government to establish Papago-Saguaro National Monument in 1914, only to withdraw the designation in 1930 at the insistence of Arizona's congressional delegation. The government subsequently divided the land among the State of Arizona, Phoenix, Tempe, and others.

ABOVE: Today the area is called Papago Park and is shared by three cities: Phoenix, Scottsdale, and Tempe. The area remained popular over the years and the Civilian Conservation Corps built trails and picnic ramadas there in the 1930s. Urban growth has somewhat infringed on the area—several roads, power lines, and canals go through and around the park. A couple of golf courses, a baseball stadium, and small patches of grass now surround the more natural desert terrain of the Buttes. Today the park includes a branch museum of the Arizona Historical Society, the Desert Botanical Garden, and the Phoenix Zoo, which is built around former fish hatchery ponds, seen here, that the state built in the 1930s. The park has paid the price for its popularity over the years, however; much of the cacti and other vegetation have been destroyed by visitors.

c. 1920

GLENDALE, LOOKING NORTH ON FIFTY-EIGHTH DRIVE

The Sine Building has been restored to its original appearance

ABOVE: This is the east side of First Avenue (Fifty-eighth Drive) in Glendale, between Glendale and Grand avenues, about 1920. The Mission-style buildings house brothers Tuck and Van Sine's hardware store and their garage. The second floor of the hardware store was a rooming house. Their brother Floyd started hardware building in 1911. He also purchased the large water tower, built by A. W. Bennett, and expanded what was Glendale's first water system before selling it to the town in 1915. The bus belonged to the private Menderson Bus Lines, which provided service to the towns outside Phoenix. Behind the Glendale State Bank, to the left, is a flagpole, which stands in the Glendale City Park. At 125 feet, it was Arizona's largest when residents installed it in 1916 as a demonstration of patriotism.

ABOVE: Glendale changed its street names in 1963 to match those of Phoenix. First Avenue is now Fifty-eighth Drive and now it stops at Glendale Avenue. The six-story building at the end of Fifty-eighth Drive (out of view here) is the Glendale Municipal Complex, finished in 1984. The complex now touches the edge of Murphy Park, formerly known as the Glendale City Park. The Velma Teague Library, which opened in 1971, sits in the middle of the park. The city removed the flagpole in 1960 and replaced it with a 100-foot one. The expansion and reconstruction of Grand Avenue changed the makeup of the street. Sine's hardware store building is still there, though the business moved about a mile away in 1991. The City of Glendale bought the Sine Building, took off the 1960s facade, and restored it for use as city offices in 1998.

GLENDALE STATE BANK

The Gillett Building still serves downtown Glendale

c. 1910

LEFT: The Glendale State Bank in the Gillett Block, located today on the southeast corner of Fifty-eighth Drive and Glendale, about 1910. Glendale was a small town northwest of Phoenix that started in 1891 as a temperance colony. The developer who established Glendale, W. J. Murphy, wanted to attract dependable farmers to the area. He formulated deed restrictions that banned alcohol in town, and in 1891 a group of settlers who belonged to the German Baptist Brethren Church—and whose members were also known as "Dunkards," for their preferred form of baptism—came to the town. The men pictured here are Dunkards; sweaters were common business clothing for the men of this church at the time. The Glendale State Bank opened in this building, built by longtime local businessman Charles L. Gillett, in 1909. Gillett (second from left) stands in front of his grocery store on the first floor.

BELOW: Today an antique store occupies the first floor of the Gillett Block. In addition to the bank, the building was the longtime home of Wood's Pharmacy. The building is now part of Arizona's largest antique district. Glendale's downtown contains some ninety antique stores and restaurants, all within walking distance of the park named after the city's founder. By the early 1970s, downtown had lost its traditional service role because of competition with new shopping malls. Glendale's leaders hoped to transform the declining district into a financial hub in the early 1980s. Instead, by the late 1980s, the area's historic buildings and the nearby historic neighborhood of Catlin Court started to attract people with a different vision of what downtown Glendale could be.

c. 1900

MANISTEE RANCH

Manistee was one of the last remaining cattle ranches in the Phoenix area

LEFT: This view of the Manistee Ranch, located about a mile north of the original Glendale town site, was taken around 1900. Wisconsin native Herbert Hamilton developed a ranch here in the 1890s and hired Glendale carpenter William Weigold to build this house for the family. Weigold completed this Queen Anne Victorian house in 1897. It featured three stories, a basement, a sleeping porch, and a veranda around the front three sides. Hamilton sold the house and the 320-acre ranch to Louis Sands, a successful lumberman and rancher, in 1907. Sands renamed the property Manistee Ranch after his hometown in Michigan. The ranch was a combination cattle-feeding operation, farm, citrus orchard, and palm grove.

ABOVE: Manistee Ranch is now a public park near the southwest corner of Northern and Fifty-first avenues. The Glendale Historical Society cares for the house and provides tours. John Sands inherited the house from his father and lived here until his death in 1993. A couple years later, the Sands family decided to develop the ranch, including the 1897 house, for residential, commercial, and retail uses. Manistee was one of the last remaining cattle ranches in the Phoenix area. Responding to an outpouring of public support to save the ranch house, a special landmark for many residents, Glendale organized a task force to save this significant property. Using state grants, the city purchased the 4.3-acre park in front of the house, and the society bought the house and another 2.2 acres. The Sands family donated $140,000 to assist the effort. The restoration of the house was completed in 2004.

1933

MILL AVENUE BRIDGE

The dedication of the bridge was marked by two days of celebrations

ABOVE: Ecstatic over finally having a dependable automobile bridge over the Salt River, Phoenix-area residents celebrated the dedication of the Mill Avenue Bridge for two days. Tempe photographer Stan Schirmacher probably caught this view of the festivities, looking south toward the bridge, downtown Tempe, and Tempe Butte, on May 1, 1933. The Hayden Flour Mill is visible to the upper right of the bridge. Presiding at the dedication was B. B. Moeur, a former Tempe doctor and the current governor of Arizona. The bridge actually opened to traffic in August 1931 but was not dedicated until much later. The Mill Avenue Bridge replaced Tempe's Ash Avenue Bridge, a smaller, damaged wagon bridge located a little to the west.

ABOVE: The Mill Avenue Bridge has remained open continuously since its completion in 1931. For many years it was the only crossing over the Salt River anywhere in the Phoenix area. Massive floods raged down the river in 1980, closing all the bridges except for Mill Avenue and one in Phoenix. Over 92,000 cars crossed the Mill Avenue Bridge in one twenty-four-hour period during that flood. The water hit the bridge at 200,000 cubic feet per second and far exceeded what the bridge was designed for, but it held. Today the Tempe Town Lake sits below the bridge, although the river still flows occasionally. The lake is part of a redevelopment project that attracted the three blue towers of the Hayden Ferry Lakeside project, among other towering structures that have been built in the area in the last twenty years. The New Mill Avenue Bridge, to the left, opened in 1994 to take some traffic off the old bridge.

TEMPE BRIDGES

Tempe Town Lake now occupies this section of the riverbed

BELOW: The Salt River is overflowing its banks, as seen from the top of Tempe Butte in Tempe, about 1931. Looking a little to the northwest, one can see Tempe's three important bridges. The bridge at the top is for the railroad, and it was rebuilt in 1909 to replace one lost in a flood. The Ash Avenue Bridge in the middle was the first wagon bridge over the Salt River in the Phoenix area. The newly completed Mill Avenue Bridge is the last of the three. The remains of a second railroad bridge can be seen below that. The Hayden Flour Mill is the tall building to the far left. Just above the left edge of Mill Avenue, Tempe Beach Swimming Pool, the largest pool in Arizona for many years, is visible. The Salt River continued to have water in it on an annual basis until the last of the upstream dams was completed in the 1940s.

c. 1931

BELOW: Today five bridges cross over the Salt River from the same vantage point. There is still water in the riverbed, but it's actually the Tempe Town Lake, which opened in 1999 as part of Tempe's Rio Salado Project—an ambitious plan to develop the land-locked city's last piece of open space. The 1912 railroad bridge is still there. The old Ash Avenue Bridge had been damaged in floods and was finally demolished in 1991. The New Mill Avenue Bridge, completed in 1994, now sits to the right of the Old Mill Avenue Bridge. Between the railroad and New Mill Avenue bridges is the Tempe Light Rail Transit Bridge. Completed in 2007, it lights up at night when trains pass over it. At the far west end of the lake is the Tempe Town Lake Pedestrian Bridge, opened in 2011. In the center is the rebuilt Tempe Beach Park, which replaced the pool.

c. 1931

ANDRE BUILDING

Fire took many of the historic structures that once stood on Mill Avenue

LEFT: This parade on Mill Avenue in Tempe is proof of the street's importance. The structure to the left is the Andre Building, once owned by local saddle maker and notorious crank Captain R. G. Andre. At this point the Masons had taken over the upper story as their meeting hall. The ground floor hosts Price Wickliffe and his furniture and undertaking business, an interesting combination. The other large building on the block is the Chipman-Petersen Building, one of the business operations of successful Danish immigrant Niels Petersen. To the right of that is the Vienna Bakery, a business started by German immigrant Charles Bauer. His family operated the bakery until the 1960s.

ABOVE: Only a few of the same buildings still stand on the block. The Andre Building is now home to Rúla Búla, an Irish pub operated by the Guinness beer company. The pub's interior was built in Ireland and shipped over in 2000. Fire took many of the historic structures that once stood on this street and also threatened the Andre Building as workers prepared for the new tenant in 1999. Most of the buildings to the right end of the block burned in the 1940s. A 1990 fire destroyed the Chipman-Petersen Building. The owner replaced it with a new building that vaguely resembles the old. Today half of the original Vienna Bakery building is still here. Mill Avenue is still a big part of community life, however. Tempe frequently closes the street to host large block parties for New Year's celebrations and art festivals.

LAIRD & DINES

DRUGS

DR

c. 1901

LAIRD & DINES BUILDING
The drugstore was Tempe's unofficial city hall

LEFT: Three men operated one of Tempe's oldest and most influential businesses. Shown here around 1901, Dr. J. A. Dines, Hugh Laird, and Laird's brother Bill are standing in front of their business on the northeast corner of Fifth Street and Mill Avenue. Dr. Dines and the Lairds opened their drugstore in 1901 in this building, which was built in 1893. Hugh trained under Dr. Dines to become a pharmacist. Both Dines and Hugh Laird served as mayor of Tempe, with a combined twenty-five years of service. Because of this, the drugstore was Tempe's unofficial city hall and many decisions were made here. The business remained open until 1964. The Laird's transformed their Victorian building to the Spanish Colonial style in 1929.

ABOVE: Today the building again resembles the Victorian structure it was a hundred years ago. Not only did the Lairds change the building in the 1920s, the state highway department expanded Mill Avenue in the early 1960s and took off the west veranda. Tempe's downtown became a low-rent district for many years until the city and private developers transformed the area into an entertainment district in the 1980s. New owners rehabilitated the Laird & Dines Building in 1994, reconstructing the veranda and corner turret. The two-story building with a basement is now home to several bars and nightclubs. Tempe renamed the intersection in front of the building Fackler Square in 2003, in honor of one of the chief planners behind Mill Avenue's renewal.

1905

TEMPE, LOOKING SOUTHWEST FROM TEMPE BUTTE
Tempe's population has grown from 1,000 to 170,000 since 1905

LEFT: Here is the town of Tempe on April 9, 1905. The view is looking southwest, and it was taken from Tempe Butte. The big road running from left to right is Fifth Street. On the right end of Fifth Street, Mill Avenue can be seen running to the south. Fifth and Mill was the heart of Tempe's business district, as evidenced by the large buildings on the corners. Tempe had a population of a little over 1,000 people in 1905.

ABOVE: Tempe has nearly 170,000 people today and doesn't have a single farm within its boundaries. The city is also land-locked and can no longer grow outward. Instead it is growing upward, as is shown here. The

skyscraper to the upper far right is the tallest building in Arizona outside of Phoenix. The thirty-story residential West Sixth II building opened in 2011 after years of recession-hampered effort. The upside-down pyramid in the center is Tempe's City Hall, built in 1970. City Hall's construction led to a renewed interest in developing the "old town" area of Tempe. A lot of that redevelopment occurred along Mill Avenue in the last forty years. A few of the original buildings are still there. Mill Avenue is a popular destination for students from nearby Arizona State University. A METRO station and light rail tracks can be seen at the bottom of the photograph. One of Tempe's oldest remaining neighborhoods, Maple-Ash, is visible in the upper center.

1915

OLD ST. MARY'S CHURCH / OUR LADY OF MOUNT CARMEL

The former barrio is now part of the Arizona State University campus

116

LEFT: This view of the intersection of Normal Avenue and Eighth Street (College and University today) is looking directly north along Normal Avenue at Tempe Butte. To the left stands St. Mary's/Our Lady of Mount Carmel church. Tempe's first water reservoir, added in 1903, is visible on the upper right of the butte. On the right side of the street sits a sprinkler wagon that would spray water on the streets to keep dust down. Normal Avenue was the boundary between Tempe's Mexican American neighborhoods, or barrios, and white Tempe. The barrio next to the church was called San Pablo, or sometimes Barrio el Centro. Father Severinus Westhoff, the Franciscan priest assigned to Tempe in 1895, wanted to unite his white and Hispanic parishioners by constructing this church between the two communities. It was completed in 1903.

ABOVE: The church and the butte remain today, but there has been a lot of change around and between them. The former barrio is now part of the Arizona State University campus. In the early 1950s, the school used eminent domain to buy the barrio. With its parish community dispersed, the Catholic Church moved further south. In 1962 the parish gave the 1903 church building to the Newman Club, a Catholic organization serving college students. The All Saints Catholic Newman Center restored the church and still uses it. The Newman Center also built the new Main Chapel, visible to the left, in 2013 to keep up with the growth of the university. Several tall buildings in the background, the College Avenue Commons (2014) to the left and the University House Apartments (2013) to the right are also the result of the university's growth. To the right is the ASU Foundation building.

1911

OLD MAIN, ARIZONA STATE UNIVERSITY
One of the most distinctive buildings on the university campus

LEFT: Former president Theodore Roosevelt speaks on the steps of the Old Main on the campus of Tempe's Normal School. Roosevelt's March 1911 visit to Arizona was to dedicate a large dam. In fact, the car that would take him to the dedication site is parked just to the right of Old Main. During his thirteen-minute speech Roosevelt proclaimed, "I believe as your irrigation projects are established, we will see 75 to 100 thousand people here." Roosevelt had long supported spending federal money in the dry West to build dams for irrigation projects, and he signed the National Reclamation Act of 1902 to make that possible. Phoenix residents showed their appreciation of his efforts by naming their dam after him. Located east of the Phoenix area, Roosevelt Dam stored Salt River water for farmers to use during the dry years, and its completion sparked a local growth spurt.

ABOVE: Roosevelt's prediction turned out to be a bit of an understatement. Today there are 170,000 people in Tempe alone, not counting the rest of the Phoenix area. Old Main is one of the most distinctive buildings on the campus of Arizona State University (what the little Normal School became by 1958). Over the years the building was used for classrooms and offices. In the 1950s, a modern, boxy-looking addition replaced the front steps. When the ASU Alumni Association completed a restoration of the building in 2000, they returned the front steps. Ironically the architect who designed the 1950s addition was one of the first to donate money toward removing it in the late 1990s. Old Main is now home to the Alumni Association and hosts numerous events in a large ballroom on the third floor.

NIELS PETERSEN HOUSE
One of the fanciest houses in the Salt River Valley

BELOW: Susana Petersen, standing in the middle, entertains winter guests in front of the Petersen House near Tempe, in around 1900. Susana's husband, Niels, was a Danish immigrant who arrived in Tempe in 1871. He built a large cattle ranch and farm and owned over 2,000 acres of land by the time he died in 1923. Niels hired a well-known local architect named James Creighton to build this Queen Anne Victorian house in 1892. Niels married Susana Decker in Pennsylvania, and he wanted her new house to be built in a style that was more familiar to her. This house replaced one made out of adobe or mud bricks and was one of the fanciest in the Salt River Valley; it could easily hold its own against some of the extravagant houses in Phoenix.

c. 1900

BELOW: Today the Petersen House is a historic house museum operated by the Tempe History Museum. The Petersens did not have children, and the house passed to Susana's nephew, Edwin Decker, when she died in 1927. Edwin and his wife, Una Belle, refurbished the house and replaced the old Victorian-style porch with a Craftsman Bungalow–style one in 1930. Decker died in 1947 and Una Belle rented the house to the family of Arizona State College art professor Tom Harter. She sold off most of the ranch by the time she died in 1968. The land became neighborhoods, strip malls, and industrial parks. Since the Deckers, too, were without heirs, the old Petersen will required the house to pass to a fraternal lodge called the International Order of Odd Fellows. The lodge gave the house to the City of Tempe in the 1980s, and the Tempe Historical Society restored it as a museum.

1964

GRADY GAMMAGE AUDITORIUM / ASU GAMMAGE

The last public commission of architect Frank Lloyd Wright

ABOVE: Here is Grady Gammage Auditorium, shortly after its completion in 1964, on the campus of Arizona State University in Tempe. Named for the university's long-time and transformative president, the building is considered to be the last public commission of architecture of Frank Lloyd Wright. Wright and Gammage were friends and in 1957 Gammage asked Wright to design an auditorium. The men walked the campus when they came to the curve where Mill Avenue turned into University Drive. Studying the

curve Wright declared "I believe this is the site. The structure should be circular in design, yes." Wright had already been asked to design an auditorium for another desert, in Baghdad, Iraq, but the assassination of King Faisal II in 1958 canceled the project. Wright modified the design for the Arizona setting. Neither man saw the completion of the project they launched, as each died in 1959. The venue hosted its first performance on September 18, 1964.

ABOVE: Now called ASU Gammage, the auditorium is a major landmark and considered one of the best venues in the western United States for Broadway shows. The auditorium continues to be a major contributor to the region's culture and entertainment. Since opening, Arizona State University expanded to several campuses in the metropolitan area and beyond. ASU's Tempe campus had over 50,000 students in 2016, ranking the campus sixth nationally for size. This is a sizeable amount for the campus's host city Tempe, which now has about 170,000 people. Because of its association with Frank Lloyd Wright, the structure went on the National Register of Historic Places in 1985—far in advance of the customary waiting period of fifty years. ASU Gammage hosted the last debate during the 2004 presidential campaign.

1932

CAMELBACK MOUNTAIN

The base of the mountain is home to some of the area's wealthiest and most famous residents

LEFT: This is Camelback Mountain, one of the Phoenix area's most distinctive and intriguing landmarks. The mountain got the name Camelback, for obvious reasons, as early as 1903, but it was also called Camelsback until the 1930s. Early on, this 2,700-foot-tall mountain became a popular place for picnicking and horseback riding. Camelback was probably the most photographed landmark in the Phoenix area's early history. Shown here in 1932, the base of the Camelback attracted farms and later citrus orchards. Farmers often planted their orchards near the base of the area's mountains. In winter, cold air rolled down the slope of the base and away from the trees, protecting the trees and their fruit from frost. At the bottom is the Arizona Canal, which provided water, the other important ingredient for growing citrus fruit.

ABOVE: The citrus orchards are mostly gone now, replaced by homes and residents attracted by Camelback Mountain's beauty. Some of these neighborhoods were built in the midst of the old orchards. Arcadia, a neighborhood started in the 1920s, encouraged homeowners to plant citrus trees on their large lots. A few of these trees survive today, although the trend lately has been to knock down the original houses and to build something much larger on the lot. The road in the middle running toward the mountain and north of the canal is Arcadia Road. Arcadia is such a desirable area in which to live that realtors have attached the name to places outside the boundaries of the original neighborhood. On the immediate base of the mountain sit homes for some of the Phoenix area's wealthiest and most famous residents.

c. 1930

CAMELBACK MOUNTAIN—PRAYING MONK

Urban growth has transformed this view of the mountain

ABOVE: This is a side view of Camelback Mountain, looking east, taken sometime around 1930. The mountain doesn't look very much like a camel from this vantage point, but the mountain's other famous feature is visible. A small jut of stone can be seen near the midway point on the left of the mountain. This is the Praying Monk, which actually does look like a kneeling person. Hikers who get closer to the feature come across a rectangular boulder balancing on one of its corners. The legend is that the monk was told not to drop his Bible or he would be turned to stone. Farms are starting to creep up to the mountain in this view, a newly cleared road runs right toward the landmark, and a wire fence stands to the right.

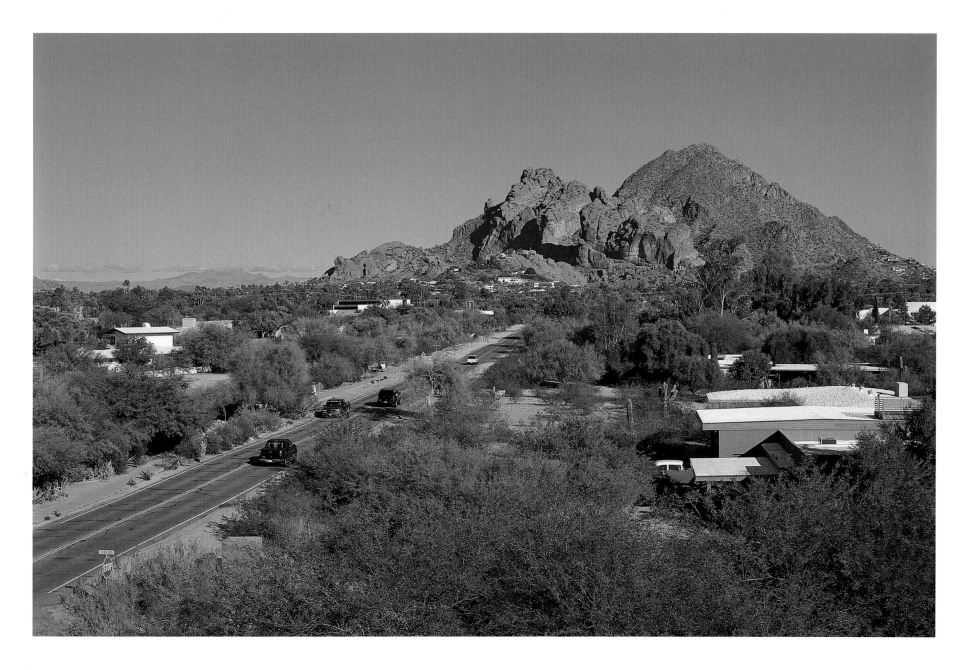

ABOVE: Today urban growth has swept around Camelback Mountain. The area west of the mountain is now part of the Town of Paradise Valley, an area of exclusive homes for the wealthy and famous. Several resorts also hug the mountain's base today. Upscale homes and fancy resorts moved toward the mountain in the late 1930s and flooded the area in the 1950s. Responding to public concern, attempts were made to limit development at the mountain's top in the 1950s. Yet none of these efforts succeeded until Barry Goldwater, Arizona senator and former presidential candidate, started a fund-raising campaign to purchase most of the remaining mountain in 1965. Using private money and public grants, the City of Phoenix bought most of the remaining open space by 1970. The Praying Monk can now be viewed by hikers in Echo Canyon Park.

c. 1930

JOKAKE INN / PARADISE INN

Built by the first Pueblo Revival architect in the Phoenix area

ABOVE: The Jokake Inn, located at the foot of Camelback Mountain, was one of the first resorts in the Phoenix area. The hotel is associated with Robert T. Evans, an engineer and architect, who visited the area frequently from his home town of Chicago. He studied the native building styles and techniques of the Southwest before moving to Arizona in 1923 with his wife Sylvia. Robert Evans designed and built the Jokake Inn

with adobe brick. Sylvia opened a tea room in it in 1926 and the couple expanded it into a hotel in 1928. Following the tone set by the bell towers' distinctive look, she decorated the place with a Southwestern theme. The Jokake Inn quickly became a popular winter resort.

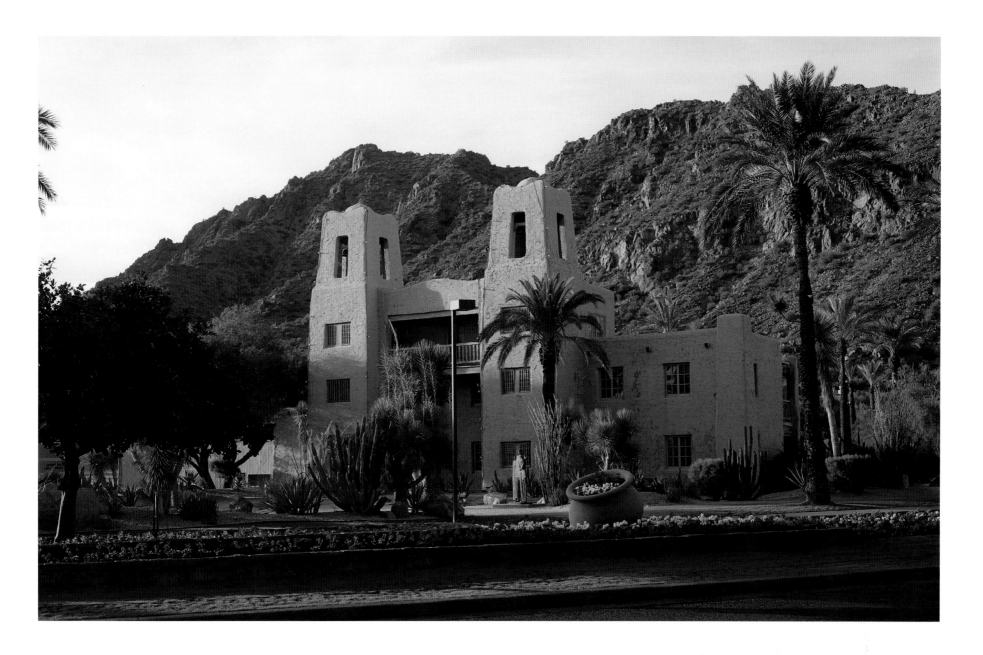

ABOVE: Now the Jokake Inn bell towers stand at the entrance of the Phoenician Resort. Sylvia and Robert Evans divorced in 1943 and she continued to operate the Jokake Inn. Robert designed and built the Paradise Inn to the immediate east. Opened in 1946, the Paradise Inn focused on outdoor activities for its winter visitors. Today Evans is recognized as a master Arizona architect and other examples of his work can still be seen in Phoenix and Tempe. The Paradise Inn is gone now except for the part of its golf course that is included in the Phoenician Resort's golf course. The luxury Phoenician Resort opened in 1988 on land that was once occupied by the Jokake Inn, the Paradise Inn, and other former resorts. Built by Charles Keating, a local developer and savings-and-loan executive, he wanted a world-class attraction but lost it because of his role in the savings and loan crisis of the late 1980s. A new owner recently renovated the Phoenician.

SCOTTSDALE ROAD AND MAIN STREET

The village of Scottsdale is now a large city

c. 1937

LEFT: This photograph shows the intersection of Scottsdale Road and Main Street, looking north, in about 1937. Located to the northeast of Phoenix, Scottsdale was just a small, unincorporated village in the 1930s and Scottsdale Road was unpaved and dusty. Earl's Grocery, located in a two-story adobe building, is on the left. Earl Shipp worked at the grocery store when it was called Byer's Market and later bought out his boss. Mort Kimsey's garage is to the right, on the northeast corner. Mort's family moved out to Scottsdale in 1915. Mort later became one of the first city councilmen when Scottsdale incorporated in 1951 and the town's second mayor.

BELOW: The intersection is today at the heart of Scottsdale's arts district. Art galleries take up the corners where Earl and Mort had their businesses. The village of Scottsdale is now a large city sprawling to the north, and Scottsdale Road is one of its major thoroughfares. Part of its early appeal came from the arrival of Western-themed artists in the 1930s and 1940s. Many of them established studios near this intersection. Later some of the artists moved a little north and started the Fifth Avenue district. The area became a popular tourist destination in the 1950s, and today art galleries and gift shops catering to tourists line Main Street.

1959

MAIN STREET, LOOKING EAST

"Where the Old West meets the New West"

ABOVE: This is Main Street in Scottsdale, looking east from Scottsdale Road. Brown Road crosses Main Street to the middle right. This was the main business district of the village of Scottsdale through the 1940s. This changed when one entrepreneur bought the town's old post office building and turned it into a Western-themed clothing store. He installed a Western-style covered sidewalk in front of his business with a fake horse above the entrance. Soon the look caught on and Scottsdale

promoted itself as "the West's most Western town." Another important part of Scottsdale's growing tourism district was the Lulu Belle Restaurant, pictured here in 1959. Owners Evelyn and Bobby Foehl gave their business a late Western or "Gay Nineties" theme complete with an "authentic Old West bar." This was one of the most popular places in Scottsdale to visit or to take visitors to.

ABOVE: The Lulu Belle Restaurant is no longer there but Main Street is still the heart of what is now called Old Town Scottsdale—"Where the Old West meets the New West." Visitors can still get a similar experience just down the road to the right at the Rusty Spur Saloon. In business since 1958, the saloon is everything tourists think a cowboy bar should be, with a rustic interior and live music. Further down on Main Street, past Brown Road, is the Scottsdale Mall, an outdoor district of stores, restaurants, and museums. The overall area contains Scottsdale's major night life and it is also a major arts center for the metropolitan area. Not surprisingly, tourism is one of Scottsdale's major industries. Over 7.5 million people visit the city annually, many of them staying in over seventy resorts and hotels stretching far to Scottsdale's north.

1963

TALIESIN WEST
Home to the Frank Lloyd Wright School of Architecture

LEFT: Famed architect Frank Lloyd Wright used Taliesin West as a winter home and base for his architecture fellowship starting in 1937. He fell in love with the Sonoran desert when he first came to Arizona in 1928. He returned in 1933 and later purchased land north of Scottsdale on the southern slope of the McDowell Mountains. His group started building a structure he called Taliesin West after his summer home, Taliesin, in Wisconsin. Wright's style was to use locally available materials to build a structure suitable for the local environment. Taliesin West was made out of "desert masonry"—local desert rocks stacked in wood frames and filled with "desert concrete" (desert sand, cement, and a little water). Also attracted to the natural light of the desert, the drafting room used translucent canvas as a roof. Wright and his apprentices continued to change and add to the building every winter season.

ABOVE: Today Taliesin West is one of two seasonal campuses used by the Frank Lloyd Wright School of Architecture. By the time of his death in 1959, Taliesin West expanded to a 10-acre compound with a private office, drafting studio, residences, dining hall, and the Cabaret Theater. His former students kept his legacy alive and they continued to care for and change the structure, replacing the canvas in the drafting room with plastic because of the intense desert sun. Concerned about the long-term preservation of the complex, the Frank Lloyd Wright Foundation formed the Taliesin West Preservation Oversight Committee. The committee released its Preservation Master Plan in 2015 which detailed "what needs to be preserved and restored and why." Taliesin West became a National Historic Landmark in 1982 and the United States nominated Taliesin West for the UNESCO World Heritage List in 2016. Over 100,000 people visit the site annually.

1913

LEHI SCHOOL

Lehi was the first Mormon settlement in the area

ABOVE: Mormon settlers out of Utah started Lehi in 1877. The Church of Jesus Christ of Latter-day Saints asked Daniel Webster Jones to establish a community in the area. Situated to the east of Phoenix and Tempe, Lehi was the first Mormon settlement in the area. They built a small fort, called Fort Utah, out of adobe bricks. The following year one of the settlers, Henry C. Rogers, donated 5 acres of land to start a school not far from the fort. A different group founded another Mormon community a little south of Lehi in 1878 on a flat piece of land that was higher in elevation. Appropriately, residents called their new town Mesa. The Lehi School District built this Neoclassical Mission Revival school, which is shown here shortly after its completion in 1913. Lehi never incorporated as a town, but the school represented Lehi's identity as a separate place.

RIGHT: The Mesa Historical Museum now uses the old school as an annex to store its collections. The town of Mesa grew and engulfed Lehi, forming a rural pocket in a vast city. A freeway now runs along the northern edge of Lehi, but doesn't go through the middle as was once planned. Mesa's school district absorbed the old Lehi School district in the 1940s and closed Lehi School in 1976. The building sat vacant for a long time because the cost of tearing it down was more than buying a new piece of land. The district turned the building over to the Mesa Historical Society in 1987, which opened a museum in the building the same year. In 1993 the society changed its name to the Mesa Historical Museum. It used the old school for a number of years, but moved the exhibits to another space in Mesa's downtown to be easier for visitors to reach.

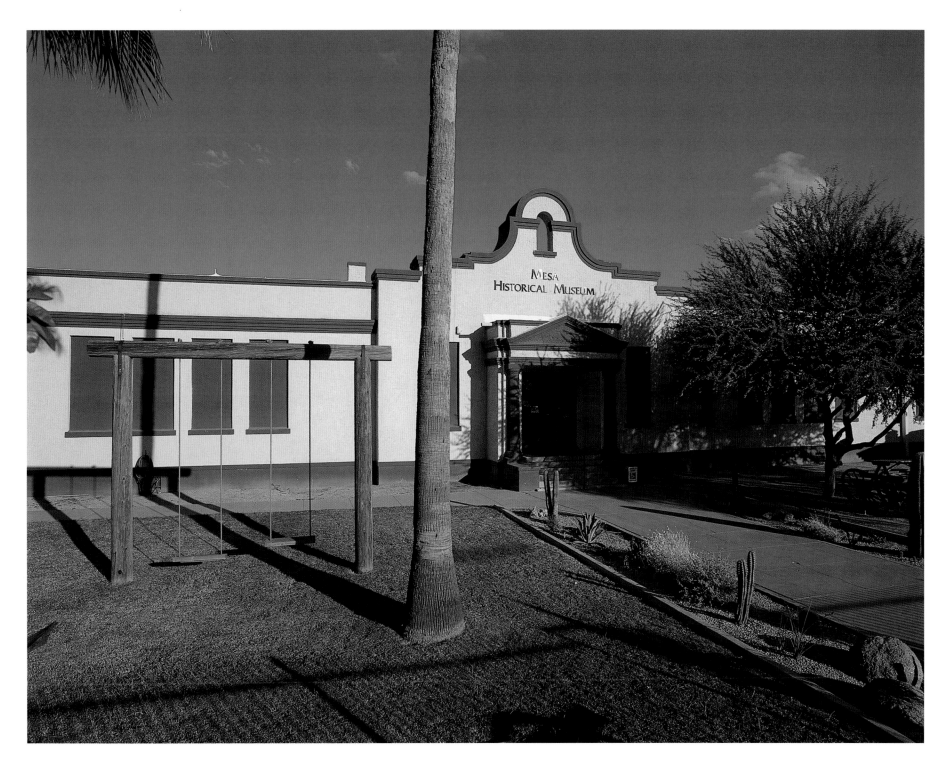

MAIN AND MACDONALD, LOOKING EAST

METRO light rail trains began serving downtown Mesa in 2015

BELOW: This is the intersection of Mesa's Main Street, the main street through town, and Macdonald around 1920. Mesa streets were famous for their width. Laws required the streets to be wide enough to turn a team of freight animals around without backing up. In 1915 this left enough room to park cars in the middle of the street.

Looking west, the building to the right is Chandler Court. Built in 1908, it claims to be one of the first buildings with evaporative cooling in the world. The tall building to the left of Chandler Court is the Pomeroy Building. Its second floor had a large hall, and it hosted many of Mesa's early social events.

c. 1920

BELOW: Acacia trees now dominate the view at street level. Mesa added these desert native trees as another unifying element for its historic business street in the 2000s. The trees also provide additional shade. Before that Mesa added a unifying arcade or covered walkway in front of many of the old businesses in the 1970s. The middle-street parking disappeared around 1940. Now METRO light rail trains use the middle of Main Street. The focus of the second expansion of the regional system, METRO trains began serving downtown Mesa in 2015. Behind the train, Chandler Court is still there. Hidden by trees, the Pomeroy Building is still there too. It still contains one of its traditional businesses—a men's clothing store. Through donations and purchases, Mesa established a large sculpture collection and displays these throughout its downtown. Some bronze statues feature the variety of people who frequented Main Street.

c. 1940

MAIN STREET, LOOKING WEST
Still a vibrant shopping district

ABOVE: Looking west, here is Mesa's Main Street in the 1940s. Some of the town's most important commercial buildings can be seen here. The man crossing the road in the middle left of the view is at Macdonald Street. To the right of the crosswalk, the building with the columns and the double parapet and spires is Chandler Court. Built in 1908 by developer and entrepreneur Dr. Alexander Chandler, who later founded the town of Chandler to the south, this was Mesa's first office building. The last tall building on the right, behind the large marquee sign, is the Pomeroy Building. Built in 1891, it is one of Mesa's oldest commercial structures. Across the street from Chandler Court is Mesa's first theater, the Nile, which started showing "talkies" in 1929. Main Street was the place for residents and regional farmers to get the groceries and goods they needed, particularly on Saturdays.

ABOVE: Today Mesa's Main Street is still a vibrant shopping district, although with more antique stores and boutiques than groceries. Main Street felt the same pressures as other traditional downtowns in the metropolitan area from automobiles and new shopping centers and malls. The former Tri-City Mall, which opened a mile west of town in 1968, started to draw away businesses and shoppers. However, Mesa has invested heavily in its downtown district with museums and art centers, and today visitors will find a variety of restaurants and shops in the area. The recently completed METRO light rail expansion also brings people into the area. Chandler Court has been enclosed and contains an antique store. The Nile Theater remains too, although it is hidden behind trees in this view. The building has again returned to its entertainment roots by offering live music. The towers to the right are a senior-living community.

The House of the Lord

Erected by the
Church of Jesus Christ of Latter Day Saints

1927

ARIZONA MORMON TEMPLE

The first Mormon temple in Arizona

LEFT: A temple is the most important building there is for members of the Church of Jesus Christ of Latter-day Saints. The temple is the sacred place where members can get married and participate in other important services. This was the first temple in Arizona, shown here shortly after its completion in 1927. Mormons, now called Latter-day Saints, first settled in Arizona in the 1860s and established Mesa in 1878. Mesa quickly became the center of the Mormon community in Arizona, yet church members had to travel to St. George, Utah—site of the nearest temple—to get married. The completed temple, located on the main road through Mesa, soon became the focus of the city.

ABOVE: The Arizona Temple is still an important place for Latter-day Saints, but it is no longer the only temple in Arizona or even in the Phoenix metropolitan area. The church built four additional temples throughout the state since 2003 and is currently building another in Tucson. The Mesa Temple was the first place where official ceremonies were performed in Spanish. The church rededicated the temple in 1975 after a major renovation. Mesa is now the third-largest city in the state, and residential neighborhoods now surround the once-isolated temple. Across the street to the west is the Mesa Family History Center, which helps thousands of people research their heritage each year.

INDEX